SALTWATER FLY TYING

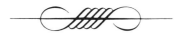

SALTWATER FLY TYING

Frank Wentink

Foreword by Dick Talleur

LYONS & BURFORD, PUBLISHERS

NEW YORK

Library of Congress Cataloging-in-Publication Data
Wentink, Frank.
Saltwater fly tying / Frank Wentink.
p.   cm.
Includes bibliographical references and index.
ISBN 1-55821-133-0 : $22.95
1. Fly tying.   2. Saltwater fly fishing.   I. Title
SH451.W48   1991
688.7'912—dc20   91-29180
CIP

Printed in the United States of America

10 9 8 7 6 5 4 3 2

TO MY WIFE, JEAN,
who has been my closest friend and companion for almost forty years;
and to our children,
CATHY, MARY JEAN, MAUREEN, BETH, and BONNIE,
who have given us so much pleasure
and several wonderful grandchildren.

ACKNOWLEDGMENTS

I wish to thank all those with whom I've dressed or cast a fly through the years—each and every one has made fly tying and fly fishing a constant learning experience. However, I must specifically mention Del Bedinotti, Bill Dorato, and the late Dud Soper. Their friendship, talent, and willingness to share have greatly enhanced my fly-fishing experience and, I hope, my tying skills.

A special thanks to Jack Fragomeni and Bob Popovics for generously sharing their tying techniques; Jack Goetke for sharing numerous fishing adventures (and innumerable misadventures); Tom Knight for his excellent photoprocessing and his willing assistance under a barrage of questions; Nick Lyons for his advice and counsel; and Linda Peterson for her superb line drawings.

Last, but not least, I would be remiss if I did not single out Dick Talleur. It was he who overcame my inertia with substantial prompting and provided me the impetus to undertake this endeavor. Then, in spite of a heavy schedule, he gave generously of his time to review the entire manuscript, and provided excellent advice on both the text and the photography.

CONTENTS

FOREWORD

Frank Wentink has been a friend and associate for a quarter of a century, and throughout this era I've greatly admired his masterful tying.

My first exposure to Frank's work involved his bass bugs. Never terribly facile with deer hair myself, I was awed by the neatness and beauty of Frank's creations, as well as their functionality. I was particularly impressed by some of the innovations he instituted—little improvements that made the flies more effective, and facilitated tying them. It was obvious that these were based on experience and trial and error; Frank is no closet tyer.

Over the years, Frank has fallen in love with the sea, and his problem-solving approach has been carried over into his saltwater tying. He spends a great deal of time fishing the ocean, and as an upstate New Yorker, has to commute to the sea. He has amassed a wealth of experience with everything from the bluefish and stripers of the northeastern coasts to the swift, powerful, and often-devastating fish of subtropical waters. His qualifications as a fly-tying expert are valid and impressive.

Frank's engineering background and his many years of experience in technically demanding work are reflected in his tying, particularly in his teaching of tying. Even with larger saltwater patterns, detail and technique are essential to efficient tying, as they are to enhanced effectiveness. In this book, Frank presents such methods to the reader with clarity and completeness. The photographic sequences are especially effective in demonstrating what's critical in the construction of a particular pattern. Even the casual tyer should have no trouble understanding and implementing what Frank presents here.

There are a lot of fly-tying books out there. This one is unique in its freshness, thoroughness, and utter practicality, and is thus a valuable addition to the tying library. I commend Frank on his excellent work and highly recommend his book to all who aspire to tie flies for the salt.

DICK TALLEUR

PREFACE

Fly fishing is one of the fastest growing participant sports in the country today. And as the interest in fly fishing grows, so does participation in fly tying. The saltwater scene leads this growth and has resulted in numerous advances in tackle and equipment. Fly tying has also benefited from this interest, with new materials, techniques, and patterns evolving, it seems, almost weekly.

Exclusive of several aborted attempts as a youngster, I've been tying flies for about thirty-five years. It's a wonderful hobby and it certainly adds another dimension to one's fishing—obviously, catching a fish on your own creation increases the satisfaction immeasurably. But there are other rewards that surpass the fishing itself. The study and the ongoing skills development are fine therapy—especially in today's hectic world—and the camaraderie and willingness to share that exists among fellow tyers is priceless. Frankly, I consider the time I've spent tying flies to be one of the best investments of my life.

Even though there are many books available on freshwater fly tying, the saltwater field has been largely neglected. It was with this in mind that I decided to write this book. It was written primarily with the intent of exposing the aspiring saltwater tyer to the techniques that will allow him or her to master most of the disciplines essential to tying today's saltwater patterns. At the same time, I know from personal experience that the flies I have chosen to include will provide the tyer with a nucleus of productive patterns for inshore fishing.

In my research, I found it difficult to pinpoint the originators of several patterns. In some cases there has been parallel development of flies, and many others have developed through step-by-step evolution. And at which color change or additional feather does a fly deserve "new pattern" status? At any rate, I have credited the developers of specific patterns where I've found them to be so recognized in other literature. In addition, I've recognized those tyers who have given me specific information about patterns they tie and their tying techniques. Much of the pleasure we derive from tying and fishing flies is because of someone else's creativity, and I believe in giving credit where credit is due. If I have made any errors in identification, I issue a blanket apology.

One note about the black-and-white photos used in the book. Materials and threads were used to give proper contrast in the completed photos. At times, these materials are obviously in conflict with the written pattern recipes, but the text is always correct.

SALTWATER
FLY TYING

1

Introduction to Saltwater Flies

Most serious anglers consider the sea to be the last frontier in fly fishing. I agree. However, many also mistakenly believe that saltwater fly fishing is a new game—and that isn't so!

Records indicate that striped bass were being taken on the fly by a handful of anglers as early as the mid-1800s. Through the ensuing years a few hardy angling pioneers continued to pursue the sport; however, it was just that—only a few, and the interest remained at a relatively low plateau for close to a century.

Then, after World War II, interest in saltwater fly fishing burgeoned. I'm not sure of the sociological reasons for this, but I feel certain it was very much related to the better pay and additional free time available to the average person in those days. At any rate, in the decade after the war, interest grew in leaps and bounds, fired by articles written by outdoor writers such as the late Joe Brooks. And in the past ten to fifteen years, that growth has accelerated dramatically. Hand in hand with the growth have been substantial advances in tackle and equipment.

Interest in fly tying has also developed rapidly and today is at an all-time high. Classes, seminars, and demonstrations are offered throughout the country by colleges and universities, in adult education classes, and by numerous fly-fishing organizations. Through participation and attendance at many of these events, I've come to realize that, although numerous books and articles have been written on freshwater flies, there is relatively little literature available on saltwater tying. This is unfortunate, because the interest is certainly there. I've found that tying a saltwater fly or displaying a few completed patterns before an audience always elicits a great deal of interest. It was this realization, along with substantial prompting and prodding by a very good angler-friend, that encouraged me to write this book.

I've met many tyers from throughout the country who are fully capable of tying their first saltwater fly—and I mean a quality product—with no prior instruction and nothing more in front of them than a pattern recipe. Yet many of these same tyers are reluctant to start. I firmly believe the major deterrent to making the transition to saltwater tying is the perception that new skills and a substantial investment in new equipment is required.

Not so! Saltwater patterns *are* different; however, the mechanics of tying them are less complicated than they are for many of their freshwater counterparts. As to equipment, an adequate start can be made with the basic tools any freshwater tyer has at hand.

Just as in fresh water, the fly design is dictated by the feeding habits and the forage on which the target fish feed. In the salt, the primary forage happens to be baitfish for most species, with a mix of crustaceans, squid, mollusks, and sea worms thrown in.

As to feeding habits, most saltwater species are constantly on the move. Very few lie in wait near cover, and there are none that rise at a given spot in a near-cadence, as is often the case in a trout stream. As a result, it's often necessary to get off a rapid-fire or change-of-direction cast in the wind as the target fish moves through the casting "window." Further, many gamefish are in the habit of following their prey before striking; consequently, a long cast and retrieve are often necessary to elicit a response. And many fish will only move to a fairly substantial mouthful.

All these factors affect fly design. Obviously, the size, appearance, and profile of the fly are important; however, it's just as important that the fly facilitate casting an adequate distance under often adverse conditions. This requires minimizing air resistance while retaining adequate size. Also, the fly design must be such that the materials do not constantly foul around the hook at the bend.

In the following chapters, I'll discuss these factors along with tools, materials, and specific fly patterns. Where appropriate, the aspects of fly design that aid casting, or at least deter it minimally, will be detailed.

Let's move first to tools and materials, and then to the actual tying. It's not my intent to impose a confining discipline on the tyer, but to present methods that work for me and many others. The average tyer will quickly adapt his or her own techniques to complete the patterns presented in the text.

Enjoy the tying! You're opening the door to a whole new world of anticipation and pleasure.

2

Tools and Materials

The average angler who has been tying flies for fresh water is well equipped to make the transition to saltwater tying. Because most saltwater flies are rather simply dressed compared to their freshwater counterparts, and because the tying mechanics are the same for both, most tyers have already acquired the requisite skills for saltwater flies. Granted, an adaptation must be made to tying flies that, on the average, are considerably larger; however, in the salt there is nowhere near the diversity of patterns as for fresh water. Once the correct proportions are attained, the tying becomes a matter of applying previously learned techniques to new pattern recipes.

The vast majority of saltwater patterns represent various species of baitfish, while most of the remainder imitate some sort of bottom-dwelling organism such as crabs or shrimp. Although some freshwater patterns imitate baitfish, the greatest portion represent the multitude of insects that abound in the freshwater environment.

Except for Atlantic salmon flies, bass bugs, and streamers, freshwater patterns would be considered quite large if tied on an 8, 6, or 4 hook. However, these are common sizes for many of the patterns used in bonefishing, and are about as small as saltwater flies go. At the other end of the scale, sizes 3/0 to 5/0, commonly used for tarpon, are practically unheard of in freshwater fly fishing. When tying flies of this size, one of the primary requisites in saltwater fly design is to retain castability. Further, much of the casting involves working in the wind and making rapid change-of-direction casts. As a result, a major design concern is that the materials do not foul around the hook gape easily. This concern can be addressed through choice of material, method of tying, or a combination of both.

Let's take a look at tools and materials for saltwater tying, focusing on those areas in which there may be substantial differences compared to freshwater tying.

TOOLS

Many freshwater tyers can make the transition to saltwater tying with no changes in or additions to their freshwater equipment. Possibly the only exception is the vise. The jaws must be large and strong enough to accept the entire range of hook sizes the saltwater tyer will encounter. That range may be from as small as #8 to 5/0 or larger.

There have been major improvements in vises in recent years, and I am hesitant to recommend any specific vise. Before you purchase one specifically for saltwater tying, I urge some study of the many models available. There are many quality vises with useful features such as an adjustable head angle, full 360-degree rotation, and interchangeable jaws. In addition, some vises can be used with either a C-clamp or pedestal-type base.

Many of the vises handle hooks from #28 to #2. The latter part of this range, sizes 8 to 2, is certainly large enough to accommodate almost all bonefish flies, many of the permit patterns, and some of the smaller streamer-type flies. However my Thompson A vise, with standard jaws, opens to about .050 inch, large enough to take some 1/0 hooks. In addition, Thompson makes Super-Jaws specifically for the saltwater tyer. They're a special-purchase jaw that retrofits easily and is designed to hold hooks as large as 6/0 securely.

There are many vises available that will accept hooks as large as size 2/0. Several require additional jaws to accommodate larger sizes. If purchasing a vise of that type, make sure jaws are available for all the hook sizes you desire—some very fine vises with interchangeable jaws will not accept the larger saltwater hooks. For example, the HMH Standard with Magnum Jaws will handle hooks up to size 6/0, but the API Spartan, a very fine vise with interchangeable jaws, does not have optional Magnum or Super-Jaws, and tops out at size 2/0.

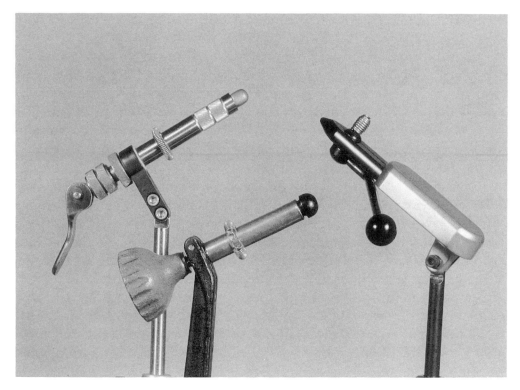

Three vises that accommodate saltwater hooks. *Left to right:* HMH Standard with Magnum Jaws, Thompson B with Super-Jaws, Regal with spring-loaded jaws.

In addition to the Thompson A and the HMH Standard, another vise I have used that will accommodate larger hooks is the Regal. There are many quality vises on the market that handle the large hooks, many of which carry a lifetime guarantee.

The HMH Standard is a superior vise for all tying, and for the serious saltwater tyer it is certainly one of the best vise choices. In addition to many excellent features, its serrated Magnum Jaws securely hold hooks from #16 through 6/0, and the additional Super Magnum Jaws holds #1 to 10/0. It's a superb-looking tool, an absolute pleasure to use, and carries a lifetime guarantee.

The Regal also carries a lifetime guarantee. It is unique in that its jaws are operated by a spring-loaded lever rather than the conventional draw collet. The one set of jaws securely holds hooks from #32 through 6/0. The smaller hooks are held in the narrow tip of the jaws, and the larger hooks are grasped back farther in the jaw where a V-shaped groove is machined in one side. The newest models are available with a rotating feature, and the head angles are adjustable.

Another vise I've used that has impressed me favorably is the Dyna-King Professional. It has many desirable features, carries a lifetime warranty, and handles hooks that range from the small dry-fly sizes to 6/0 saltwater and larger.

With some thought and ingenuity, even some of the less-costly vise models can be made to accommodate a larger range of hooks. One of my favorites is the Thompson B vise. I had mine modified to accept the Super-Jaws—or, more correctly, the jaws were modified to fit the vise. The B vise is a draw-collet model. But instead of being operated by a cam-lever mechanism, the jaws are opened and closed with a large, threaded, hand-operated nut.

Because Thompson's interchangeable jaws are made for their cam-lever vises, the jaws are not threaded, and therein lies the rub. When I purchased the jaws, I thought it would be a simple matter to cut a thread with a standard metric or American Standard die. Not so—the threads are not standard! I ended up having a toolmaker cut the threads on a lathe. Even at that, the jaws had to be annealed prior to machining and afterwards retempered to the proper hardness. By that time, I had so much invested in the vise I decided to go for the whole nine yards, and had a welder renovate the C-clamp base so it now opens a full two and a quarter inches. For me it was worth it. I tend to be heavy-handed when working with the large hooks, and I've never had a hook slip in the modified B vise. With the rapidly expanding interest in saltwater tying, I think the D. H. Thompson people are missing a bet by not marketing Super-Jaws for their B vise.

The only other tools I consider necessary are scissors, bobbin, hackle pliers, and dubbing needle. There are others that may be desirable, and I'll discuss them subsequently. But for now let's take a brief look at the essential tools, focusing on characteristics that are especially necessary for saltwater tying.

To my mind, the most important of all fly-tying tools are scissors. After all, flies can be tied without a bobbin, hackle pliers, even without a vise, but scissors are a must. If you are equipped only with fine scissors for delicate work on smaller flies, the heavier materials and larger quantities used in saltwater tying will ruin them in a hurry. The work of saltwater tying consists almost entirely of cutting synthetic hairs, bucktail, calf tail, large hackle feathers, and mylar-like materials; consequently, heavy-duty scissors, preferably with finely serrated blades, are the best for this work. The fine serrations hold slippery hair for the cutting action, and don't let the material constantly slide away from the shearing point. I keep an older pair of fine scissors available for the occasions when precise work is required.

Any bobbin used for freshwater tying will suffice for the larger saltwater flies. But if you're in the market for an additional bobbin, I'd suggest trying one with a long tube. In saltwater patterns, especially the larger ones, a great deal of material is often fastened at the bend of the

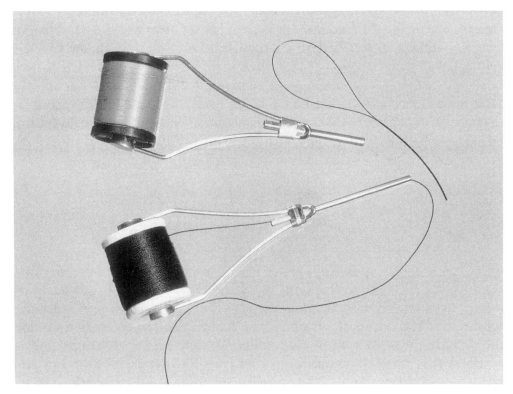

Top, Short-tube; and *bottom,* long-tube bobbin, and a floss threader.

hook. Longer bobbins provide more reach, and make it slightly easier to work around the rear portion of a long shank.

As to bobbin threaders, they're fine. However, I use floss threaders, which are available in the dental-hygiene sections of most pharmacies. They're a smooth monofilament-like loop, and a box of a dozen or so costs about one dollar.

Hackle pliers are not an absolute necessity, but they do make winding hackle considerably easier, and are convenient for holding one end of a feather while you are folding it. And they're certainly handy to hang on a thread or hackle stem to prevent unraveling in the event of breakage.

As to dubbing needles, the average tyer probably has several, either purchased or homemade, and they're used for the same purposes as in freshwater tying: applying head cement, freeing trapped hackle barbules, and so on.

There are other tools that are nice to have, but they are far from essential. I don't mean to downplay their importance or utility; I learned to tie with a minimum of equipment and have just never completely adapted to all the gadgets available. These include whip-finishers, half-hitch tools, hackle guards, tweezers, hair stackers, and combs. Any of these used for freshwater tying will suffice for saltwater flies. The only two I use are the stacker and comb. I use the stacker minimally, prefer-ring the naturally tapered appearance of most hair. I use the comb regu-larly to clean the underfur from natural hair and to untangle some of the synthetic hairs.

One last item I would suggest, although it's perhaps not actually a tool, is poster board or mat board to be used as a tying background. It masks distractions, provides a uniform contrast behind the fly, and mini-mizes eye strain during long tying sessions. Although I prefer light green, any light color with a nonglare finish would be satisfactory.

MATERIALS

The materials used for saltwater tying are basically the same as those used for freshwater; however, most are scaled up in size. Larger bucktail, longer synthetic hair, and longer and wider hackle feathers are com-monly used. In addition, although the materials themselves are similar, their characteristics vary substantially. For example, although hackle feathers are one of the major ingredients in both types of tying, I do not know of any saltwater fly that calls for the high-quality dry-fly hackles used for trout flies. Both styles of tying call for mylar or other tinsel-like materials, but while mylar is commonly used in saltwater flies, its use, comparatively speaking, is somewhat limited in freshwater patterns.

When tying flies for some saltwater species, one must accept the fact that the life of the fly can be very short. There are things that can be done in tying to make a fly less fragile than normal (I started to say "make it tougher," but I feel this wording is misleading). When fishing for species such as barracuda or bluefish, the fly should always be considered ex-pendable. Once, when I was plug-casting, my brand-new solid wooden plug, specifically designed for salt water, was bitten in two by a twenty-five-pound barracuda. If the attachment eye and hooks had not been wired together through the body, the fish would have escaped with the rear half of the plug. On another occasion, I saw a plastic saltwater plug broken into three pieces by a barracuda weighing thirty-five pounds. It would be most difficult to tie a fly that could withstand that magnitude of destructive power. However, flies can be made more durable by sub-stituting different materials or providing some sort of protection for those that are fragile.

Not all species are that destructive, but for those that are known to annihilate a fly in short order, it's often advisable to dress the fly as simply as possible while still maintaining its productivity. In subsequent chapters we will tie a very simple fly designed especially for barracuda, along with a sand eel pattern and a foam-bodied popper for bluefish.

One method that is often used to protect fragile body material such as mylar or tinsel is to overwrap it with Body Glass, V-Rib or Swannundaze—all soft, see-through plastic materials. They're usually oval in cross section, or flat on one side, and are available clear or in a variety of transparent colors. After being tied on, they're wound over the underbody in neat, contiguous wraps. Another method sometimes used to strengthen shouldering material such as a mallard or teal feather, is to coat it with clear silicone glue or Pliobond, the same procedure that is often followed in freshwater tying.

Probably the most common method of increasing durability is through substitution of materials. Bucktail or calf tail is often used in place of feathers, and where even greater durability is desired, synthetics such as FisHair or Ultra Hair are used. I wouldn't make a drastic change in materials if I felt that the productivity and overall appearance of the fly would be seriously compromised. For surface lures, closed-cell foam is often used in place of cork for popper bodies.

Hackle feathers are intended to present a relatively long, slim profile. And whether tied in as a streamer wing, or palmer-wound, they should work, or breath, easily in the water. Both saddle and spade hackles are commonly used. They should be supple but not so limp that they constantly foul around the hook.

Hair is also employed as a winging material, with calf tail commonly used on smaller flies such as those tied for bonefish. Bucktail is used for the longer wings on streamer-type flies. When wing length is to be greater than four or five inches, about the maximum length provided by the largest bucktail, synthetics such as FisHair or Ultra Hair are substituted. The synthetics are readily available in lengths up to ten inches, wear well, and are easy to work with. In addition, they come in myriad colors and shades.

Mylar is used in many saltwater patterns. The material is tough, easy to apply, nontarnishing, and is available in many colors. One of my favorites is pearlescent—it lends a subtle but noticeable sparkle to any fly. Silver, of course, is a very popular color. A decided advantage of silver mylar is that the other side of the strip is usually gold; thus one spool provides both colors.

Mylar also comes in many widths, and when using it to wrap a body, I prefer it to be 1/16 of an inch wide. It's narrow enough for a smooth, neat body, and wide enough to cover efficiently. Mylar is often mixed with or added to winging materials and should be narrow and supple for that purpose: 1/32 inch is satisfactory, 1/64 is definitely better.

There are a few new kids on the mylar block: Flashabou, Krystal Flash, and Crystal Hair. They're available in many colors and are excellent substitutes for the mylar used in wings. Of the three, Crystal Hair is probably the finest, and, like the others, it's easy to work with.

There is one other innovation I must mention—the use of epoxy or other similar materials to form the body of a fly. To the best of my knowledge, the concept and methodology started in saltwater tying and is spreading to freshwater. The fly itself looks very much like a jig; however, the fact that epoxy, rather than lead, is molded or cast around the hook makes this a fly-rod lure. Generically, this is called an epoxy fly, and we'll tie one in a subsequent chapter. Suffice to say that the body materials most commonly used are liquid epoxy, paste-type epoxy, and hot glue. I also use a water-soluble liquid latex rubber and am pleased with the results.

Those of you who are top-water enthusiasts will be happy to know that poppers are often effective in salt water. They're made exactly the same as they are for fresh water, except—and I hate to say it—larger! Cork, balsa wood, and closed-cell foam are all used, with the latter growing very rapidly in popularity. The types of synthetic foams are Evasote, Ethafoam, Live Body, Poly Foam, and several others. The advantages are buoyancy, lightness, and the ease with which they are shaped. They're also tough, and being resilient, are realistic to the touch. Molds are now available to make preshaped foam popper bodies, and preshaped cork bodies for saltwater poppers are also available, just as they are for freshwater tying. In fact, cork bodies can be purchased already mounted on the hook, and all that's required to complete the fly is to paint the body and add materials.

Threads are essential to our hobby. Without them we might glue flies, mold them, cast them, or even carve them, but we just couldn't tie them. The threads used in the salt are virtually the same as those used in fresh water, except that they're usually heavier. I use 2/0 nylon and 3/0 Monocord. Two new threads on the scene are Kevlar and polyester Unithread. The Kevlar is extremely strong, but it's slippery, tends to spread and lay flat, and is somewhat stiff. However, with some improvement I'm sure it will be a leading contender for honors in heavy-duty tying. I've just been introduced to Unithread, and it appears to be very good. It's available in several sizes, many colors, and comes waxed and plain. I would imagine its use for all types of tying will be widespread in the near future.

I probably use 2/0 nylon more than any other thread. It's strong, and is a twisted thread that doesn't flatten on the hook, and resists fraying if rubbed against the hook point. It's available in numerous colors.

Monocord is also an excellent thread for heavy tying. It's available in sizes A and 3/0, with the finer 3/0 being strong enough for all tying. The thread tends to be slippery and lies flat on the hook. It is made up of multiple strands and tends to fray easily on contact with the hook point.

On occasion I use a heavier nylon thread, size A, C, or even D, for special applications. When making up large poppers, I use the heavy thread for its greater diameter, not its additional strength. The thread is spiraled on the hook shank, rather than wrapped in contiguous turns, in the area over which the body is to be installed. The larger-diameter thread creates more room between the hook shank and the popper body, allowing more space for a heavier or more substantial glue line. I use a quick-drying epoxy to cement the body in place. Epoxy doesn't shrink during drying and effectively fills the voids created by the spiraled thread. When using finer thread, I often find that the body forces the glue out as it's slid into place over the hook.

While on the subject of glue, head lacquer is a must. However I would urge that quick-drying epoxy or super glue be used on highly stressed areas, and certainly as a final coating over the head. When using epoxy, apply it in a very thin coat with a dubbing needle. If a thicker coating is needed, apply it in multiple layers. Epoxy is heavy, and if it is applied too thickly it will run to the bottom of the hook, leaving an unsightly glob of translucent, rock-hard glue. The super glues are excellent, but follow manufacturer's instructions carefully.

The most popular hook for the salt is the Mustad Model 34007. It's made of stainless steel to resist the corrosive action of salt water, and is available in sizes 8 to 11/0. The hook is forged, has an O'Shaughnessy bend, straight shank, and ringed eye. Mustad also manufactures a similar hook, the Model 3407, that is made of carbon steel and is cadmium-plated and tinned. The Mustad 3408B is the same as the 3407 except that it has a turned-down eye. The only difficulty with the plated and tinned hook is eventual corrosion, which causes fly discoloration. On the other hand, although the manufacturers may say otherwise, I think carbon steel hooks are stronger, sharpen more easily, and hold their edges far better.

Eagle Claw's Model 254SS is another very popular hook. It is stainless steel and is similar to Mustad's 34007 except for a slightly shorter shank. Their 254N (nickel) and 254 CAT (plated and tinned) are also fine hooks.

I use jig hooks quite frequently, especially in smaller sizes for bonefish. Bones are often fished in very shallow water and an inverted tie is used to get the hook point to ride up. The eye placement on a jig hook in relation to the shank is much like that on a keel hook. An inverted tie (that is, the materials are tied on the bottom of the shank rather than the top), when used in conjunction with a jig hook almost guarantees that the hook point will ride upright. Mustad makes several jig hooks that are satisfactory for the salt. Their 34185 is cadmium-plated and tinned and is available in sizes 4 to 8/0; and their 34184 is the same but with a longer shank. It's available in #6 to 8/0.

As interest in saltwater fly fishing grows, so will the availability of various hooks. In fact, in perusing the latest catalogs, I note that some dealers are now offering stainless-steel hooks with long shanks for streamers. Another hook, the Mustad 7766, is called a Special Tarpon Hook. One I would like to see offered is a saltwater hook with a looped eye. The doubled wire behind a looped eye makes an excellent platform for lead eyes and bulky tying materials; however, it should be tapered to avoid excessive width.

Mustad's 34011 is a streamer hook with a ⅜-inch-longer-than-usual shank, and is certainly welcome to many of us who have been hoping to see such a hook for years. It's available in sizes 8 through 4/0. Just as in fresh water, it permits the tyer to proportion the fly more realistically for many streamer-type patterns, and the longer shank places the business end of the hook closer to the rear portion of the fly. In fact, in the past some saltwater tyers have resorted to using heavy-duty freshwater streamer hooks for bluefish to take advantage of the longer shank. They feel the longer shank, especially in combination with a pattern heavily dressed at the bend, minimizes the necessity for a wire leader. The design often works very well, but there are days when the fish take the fly more deeply or hit it closer to the front end, and then the only solution is a short length of wire or heavy monofilament shock leader. Many anglers carry flies made up in advance with two- or three-inch wire leaders already attached. Others opt for a ten- to twelve-inch length of sixty- or eighty-pound test monofilament.

I'm certain we're approaching an era of specialization during which a far greater selection of hooks will be made available to the saltwater fly tyer—and it's all to our advantage.[1]

Let's get on with the tying, and as we progress through subsequent chapters, more specific information will be offered about hooks, threads, and materials.

---

[1]As this book nears publication, I've just been introduced to various saltwater hooks manufactured by Partridge and by Tiemco. I have tied several flies on them and they appear to be of excellent quality.

3

The Blonde Series

I feel it's appropriate that we begin with a type of fly on which most tyers of my generation have cut our teeth, that is, the fly with which we started our saltwater fly-fishing careers. Actually, it's not one pattern, but a series of streamer-type flies known collectively as the "Blondes."

This fly type is a creation of the late Joe Brooks, and although the design is thirty-five or forty years old, it's still productive, despite the recent advances in saltwater tying. I never had the pleasure of meeting Joe Brooks, but he was responsible for introducing me and countless other fly fishers to the joy and excitement of challenging the salt with a fly rod. His writings fired up my imagination, and as a result of his stories, I realized that I could share in such wonderfully exciting fishing adventures.

By way of reinforcing my previous statements about the fly's productivity and its launching many saltwater careers, I must tell you that my first fly-caught saltwater fish, a striped bass, was taken on one of the Blondes. The fly did well for me on many occasions and kept me coming back for more.

I was aware that stripers spawned in the Hudson River in large numbers. Further, herring ascend the river in the spring on their annual conjugal journey from the ocean with the stripers following in hot pursuit.

Both species move upriver as far as the federal dam at Troy, New York, about 150 miles above Manhattan. The river at that point is not even brackish, but there is a four- to five-foot tide, with the tidal cycle occurring twice daily. In sailor's parlance, many of the fish, both stripers and herring, "lock-through" the dam with the barges and pleasure boats to the upper reaches of the Hudson River and the Mohawk River. Once they're above the dam they're in a nontidal environment and the only way they can return to the salt is via the locks at Troy. I've often suspected that some of them, perhaps many in fact, remain landlocked.

Unfortunately, the water above the dam has been closed to fishing for several years because of industrial pollution (just one more reason to oppose the polluters, and the politicians by whose tacit sanction they exist). I fished the area for several years before its closure and know it to be an excellent fishery, especially for smallmouth bass, striped bass, and several species of panfish. In addition, some sections offer outstanding fishing for largemouth bass, northern pike, pickerel, and walleye. Much of the water is wadable or accessible with a light boat or canoe, and the fish take flies readily. School-size stripers are present through most of the summer and into early fall, and at times the fishing is *really* hot! This is especially so during late summer and early fall when they feed on the newly spawned herring fry that are descending the river in shoals on their way to the ocean.

At any rate, after reading one of Joe Brooks's stories, I tied several Blondes in different colors. Knowing that the stripers follow the adult herring into the tributaries, I headed for one of the many streams that feed the lower Hudson—the tidal area below the dam. I chose a stream that I knew was wadable yet still of adequate depth for fishing at all stages of the tide.

Inasmuch as a blue-and-white lure has always been one of my favorites when plugging for stripers, I started by fishing the Argentine Blonde, a streamer of that color combination. I fished the last few hours of a rising tide and through high slack water with no further reward than a few smallmouth of rather modest proportions. But an hour or so after the tide had turned and the water was flowing strongly, the activity increased. I could see minnows and herring darting about, with schools of minnows breaking the surface in an obvious state of panic. On almost every cast that landed within a few feet of a surface disturbance I had a solid hit as soon as I started the retrieve, and I landed four or five nice smallmouth. Then I saw a washtub-size swirl behind a school and dropped the fly about five feet beyond it. I started my retrieve in one- to two-foot erratic strips and had only taken in a few feet when the line stopped dead. I raised the rod to set the hook and the line was jerked from my hand as the fish started a commanding run downstream. It ran about fifty yards before it breached the surface, and I saw the multiple stripes on the silver body. My first striper on a fly! I was ecstatic—and even more so when I landed it about fifteen minutes later. It was a nice fish, probably about eight pounds and beautifully marked.

I've since duplicated that feat many times; however, it is really hit-or-miss fishing. When the fish are in the tributaries, they're there to feed and usually hit quite readily. At times they take poppers well, but streamers are usually more effective. They're not always there, though: Having easy access to the main river, they spend more time in the big water where there's plenty of cover and lots of food. You may fish a specific stream a half-dozen times without taking a fish—that is, a striper—and then on the next trip hit a bonanza.

Later in the year, when striped bass are feeding heavily on herring fry, they can be very selective, and size becomes far more critical than color or pattern. It's usually necessary to closely match the size of the forage fish, with a difference in length of one-quarter inch often spelling the difference between success or failure. If the right-size fly is not available, one size smaller will often take fish, while a larger fly will result in repeated refusals.

One must also watch the tides, not only for fishing success, but for access to the water and safety. Both water depth and current can change drastically with the rise and fall of the tide, so that an area that's relatively placid and easily waded at one stage may be running a strong current or be well over one's waders a few hours later. When boat fishing, you may find easy access to an area at high tide, and a few hours later find yourself stranded. In fact, my first purchase every spring is a set of tide tables for the area, and I plan my fishing around them.

Although I've since landed many fish far bigger than that first striper while fishing the salt, some of the details are clouded in my memory. But that first catch, and especially the first glimpse of that line-sider flashing in the sun, is etched in my mind forever.

Before we tie our first fly, there are a couple of points I want to make. Saltwater fly tying is not encumbered with much of the formality and convention that surrounds freshwater tying, but is wide open to experimentation. In fact, I'm not sure we should use the word "pattern" when describing many saltwater flies—perhaps we should refer to them as a "type," "design," or "class." A good example is the Deceiver, which we'll tie in a subsequent chapter. That fly is tied in many colors and sizes. It's also tied with or without topping and with or without mylar in the wing. In addition, some tyers even add a shoulder with painted eyes. However, a Deceiver is a Deceiver, no matter what the personal innovations, as long as it follows concepts of the basic design.

This is also true of the fly we're about to tie. Although I've never seen any of the Blonde series tied in orange-over-white, if I told a saltwater tyer that I successfully fished a Blonde with an orange-over-white wing, he or she could easily duplicate the fly with no further description.

ARGENTINE BLONDE

GENERAL DESCRIPTION

The fly is a streamer-type or minnow-like imitation, with a silver mylar body and two bucktail wings. The rear wing, or tail, is tied on at the bend of the hook with the bucktail extending straight back one and one-half to two lengths of the hook shank. This rear wing obviously adds length to the fly, and just as important, prevents the forward wing from fouling around the bend of the hook during change-of-direction casts or when making long casts crosswind. The forward wing is tied in behind the eye of the hook and is cocked upward slightly, giving the fly depth in the vertical dimension. Because this wing is cocked upward, it tends to pulsate in a vertical plane, creating an enticing action as it's stripped through the water.

DRESSING AND COMPONENTS

Hook:	Mustad 3407 (tinned) or 34007 (stainless), #2 to 3/0
Thread:	Black 3/0 Monocord or 2/0 nylon
Body:	Silver mylar
Rear Wing (Tail):	White bucktail
Forward Wing:	Medium blue bucktail

TYING STEPS

1.   Place the hook in the vise as shown, burying the point or not, as you prefer. Breakage is not usually as much a concern as with freshwater hooks because of the heavier wire of saltwater hooks. However, if you let the hook point protrude, it quickly will become second nature to work around it, which provides better access for tying on the greater amounts of materials often used in saltwater flies.

2.   Tie the thread on a short distance behind the eye of the hook and wind it evenly in closely spaced turns back to the bend.

3.   Cut off a small bunch of white bucktail for the rear wing. This hair should be long enough so the tip ends will be one and a half to two

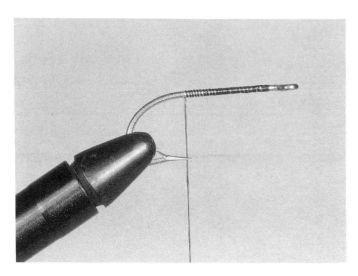

Thread tied in and
wound back to bend.

shank lengths beyond the bend of the hook, and the butt ends extend to
or beyond the eye. The bunch of hair for hook sizes 2 to 1/0 should be a
bit greater than the diameter of a wooden match, while for larger hooks
the wing should be correspondingly heavier. Do not, however, tie the
heavier wing on in one large-diameter bunch. Even though the wing is all
one color, it's a good idea to obtain the additional bulk with two or three
successive layers of hair. Thus, the thread presses on more individual
hairs, making it more difficult for them to pull out during fishing. Durability is enhanced substantially by applying a coating of head lacquer or
super glue after each layer.

4.   Prior to tying the wing in place, pull shorter hairs out with your
fingers, and pick out any extraneous unruly fibers that do not run true to
the bunch or are much longer than average. Excessive underfur is best
removed with a fine-toothed comb. If you wish, you can even up the tips
with a hair tamper, but don't overdo it. A slightly tapered effect at the
rear of the wing has a pleasing appearance.

5.   Secure the white bucktail on top of the hook at the bend with
several turns of thread.

6.   Now secure the butt ends of the hair to the top of the hook by
bringing the thread forward in evenly spaced turns around both hair and
hook. Stop at a point just behind where the thread was originally tied on.
The turns of thread do not have to be contiguous, but they should be
close enough together to provide a smooth, even base for the mylar.

7.   After binding the bucktail in place, cut the butt ends of the hair
at an angle, tapering toward the eye of the hook.

8.   Cover this slanted area with thread, maintaining the angle of the
cut. This will provide a slanted foundation for later installation of the
forward wing, and will help to maintain it in a cocked position. After covering the area, bring the thread back to a point just behind the taper,

The tail or lower wing with butt ends secured to top of shank.

The forward end of bucktail, cut at an angle and covered with thread to create a slanted foundation for the forward wing.

positioning it for tying on the mylar. It's a good idea to coat the thread and hair back to the bend of the hook with head lacquer. This will make the fly more durable and prevent the bucktail from twisting around the hook shank.

9. Tie in the mylar just behind the slanted area with the silver side out, and start wrapping toward the rear. Wrap in such a manner that the edge of the mylar neatly abuts the edge of the previous wrap, making sure that neither the hair nor the thread show through. It may be helpful

Mylar tied in just be-
hind slanted area.

Mylar is wound back
to the bend and then
forward over itself.

to barely overlap the previous wrap and then carefully slide the overlap
off.

10.   After reaching the point at the bend where the rear wing was
tied on, start wrapping the mylar forward over the first layer, again making sure the turns are contiguous. Secure the mylar at the point of tie-on
with several tight wraps of thread. Then position the thread at the front
end of the slanted area in preparation for installation of the forward
wing. Coat the mylar with glue or head lacquer for durability.

Alternate method. The shorter forward wing enhances pulsation during the retrieve.

The completed fly. The forward wing is standard length, extending to the end of the tail or lower wing.

11.   For the forward wing, cut off a small bunch of blue bucktail of the same diameter as that for the rear wing. The standard pattern calls for the forward wing to extend to the same point as the rear wing. However, I prefer it to be a little shorter than standard, so that it only extends to a point between one-half and three-quarters the length of the rear wing. This influences it to remain in the cocked position, and the fly appears to be more full-bodied vertically, and pulsation is accentuated. On the other hand, when both wings extend to the same point, they tend to cling together in the water.

12.   Tie the wing on over the slanted area with tight wraps, working toward the rear. As the thread approaches the top of the slant, check to see that the wing is cocked enough. If it isn't, take one or two turns of

thread behind the wing to raise it into proper position. Do not go beyond the slant, or these additional wraps will pull the wing back down. When satisfied, wrap forward to the point of tie-off.

13. Taper the head as required, whip-finish, and apply lacquer. After the lacquer has dried, the application of a light coat of quick-drying epoxy or super glue will substantially increase durability.

In addition to the blue-and-white of the Argentine Blonde, there are several other color combinations that are considered more or less standard. These are:

Pattern Name	Rear Wing	Forward Wing
Platinum Blonde	White	White
Honey Blonde	Yellow	Yellow
Black Blonde	Black	Black
Pink Blonde	Pink	Pink
Strawberry Blonde	Orange	Red
Irish Blonde	White	Green

As previously mentioned, there are many possible color variations in the Blonde series, with the combinations limited only by the tyer's imagination. However, a Blonde is a Blonde is a Blonde. . . .

ADDITIONAL OPTIONS

An option commonly used by many tyers is the addition of a few narrow strips of mylar to each side of the rear wing. I like this myself, but feel it can be overdone, especially if the fly is to be used on the gin-clear flats that exist in many tropical areas. On a fly like this, I use mylar sparingly. If I expect to use the fly in the tropics, I prefer the rather subtler sparkle of pearlescent mylar to the bright flash of silver.

Some tyers use Flashabou rather than mylar in the wing, while others use Krystal Flash or Crystal Hair. The many-faceted surfaces of those two latter materials reflect light under the poorest conditions.

Another very common variation is to use gold mylar for the body. In this case, gold is usually substituted in the wing also.

4

The Deceiver

The Deceiver is one of my favorite flies. It's not an exquisite pattern like many of the salmon flies, nor is it especially challenging to tie—on the contrary, it's relatively simple. I'm sure much of its appeal is due to its productivity; however, it's also admired for its innovative yet practical design. A side view offers a minnow-like silhouette, while from the top the fly is thin and straight, somewhat like the edge of a knife blade. As a result, the fly cuts through the air when cast and sinks well for its size. Further, the manner in which it is tied minimizes the possibility of materials fouling around the hook during casting while also causing the fly to undulate through the water in a lifelike manner during the retrieve.

I truly enjoy tying the fly, not only in anticipation of fishing it, but because I get a certain satisfaction as I see the minnowish configuration start to evolve as the fly is built step by step.

I first used the fly many years ago while fishing in the Everglades near Ochopee, Florida. I was walking the banks of the canals and casting to tarpon that were rolling almost constantly. I was well into my second day of incessant casting and had gone through numerous patterns without a touch. To say I was completely frustrated would be a gross understatement. On top of that, this was supposed to be a family vacation, and my wife was threatening divorce if I didn't spend more time with her and the kids. At any rate, I made up my mind I'd give it just one more hour, and then, no matter what, close up shop for the remainder of the trip. I decided to tie on a red-and-white Deceiver and stick with it, rather than waste precious moments constantly changing flies and rebuilding leader tippets.

On about the sixth cast, the rod was almost yanked from my hands in the direction of what appeared to be a geyser. The eruption occurred halfway across the canal, about thirty-five feet in front of me, and was caused by what seemed to me to be a huge tarpon. I couldn't tell if the tarpon had caused the geyser or if the explosive force of the geyser had launched the tarpon. I don't know how I hung on or how the leader held. On the second eruption, with the fish catapulting into the mangroves on the opposite bank, I pulled back and unceremoniously dumped the tarpon on its back. The tippet should have popped, but didn't.

I pulled the same stunt another four or five times, and then finally landed the startled fish, a baby tarpon of perhaps twenty pounds. Obviously, it was the grace of Our Maker that brought the fish to hand, not any skill on my part. I'm certainly glad there were no witnesses to the bout.

To vindicate myself, at least partially, I must tell you I don't even have a picture of that fish, my first tarpon ever! The camera was in the car about a hundred yards away, and I didn't want to take a chance of the fish dying for the sake of a photo. I never have been a killer, and even in my glory days of bass and trout fishing never brought home more than enough for one meal. Now it's a rarity for me to bring any home at all. Fish are too valuable a resource and have given me too much pleasure.

In retrospect, having since landed several (and lost innumerable) tarpon of all sizes, I fully realize it was the combination of the fish's relatively small size and the action of the rod I was using that saved the bacon for me that day many years ago. I was into large wind-resistant bugs for largemouth bass at that time, and using a rod with a slow casting cycle. Considering the soft action of that rod, I believe the only way I could have landed the fish, had the water been much deeper or the fish five pounds heavier, would have been to throw the rod down on the grass and bring the fish in hand over hand.

Since that time I've fished the same area on a few other occasions and landed more baby tarpon, along with snook, jack crevalle, ladyfish, and channel bass, or "reds," as they are called locally. However, I recently returned to Ochopee to try my hand at tarpon, but found it to be posted against fishing by the water-supply district. And so it seems to go in most populous areas—water shortages, pollution, overfishing, or destruction of fish habitat. Shades of my beloved Mohawk and upper Hudson rivers.

As far as I am concerned, the Deceiver, which was created by Lefty Kreh, should be in every fly fisher's arsenal. When tied in varying sizes and colors and fished with fly lines of various densities, it's certainly as productive as any fly in the salt. And don't forget to tie up some for fresh water. I said a Blonde is a Blonde, and so a Deceiver is a Deceiver. Well, a minnow is a minnow—and freshwater fish like minnows as well as their saltwater counterparts. Just tie them the appropriate sizes.

The Deceiver is tied in many colors, so let's start with one of the most popular, a red-and-white, and we'll dress it up with a peacock-herl topping.

RED-AND-WHITE DECEIVER

GENERAL DESCRIPTION

The Deceiver is a streamer-type fly with several relatively long hackle feathers tied on at the bend of the hook to form the rear half of the fly. These feathers are parallel to one another, tied dull-side to dull-side; they do not splay outward, and they extend straight back, usually one to two hook lengths. Several strips of mylar are added to each side of the fly outside the hackles to provide some flash, and then a mylar body is wound on, covering the shank from the bend to a point behind the eye, leaving enough room for a collar. The collar, usually bucktail or calf tail, is tied on next in the space provided. It's tied on in a manner that distributes it around the hook so that it flows back and merges with the feathers to complete the minnow-like profile. The topping, if used, is added next.

The positioning of the feathers at the bend adds length to the fly and minimizes the chances of fouling during a cast. Being tied on dull-side to dull-side causes them to cling together and accounts for the relative lack of air resistance during casting and the lifelike movement during the retrieve.

DRESSING AND COMPONENTS

Hook:	Mustad 3407 (tinned) or 34007 (stainless), #6 to 4/0
Thread:	White, black, red, or matching color, 3/0 Monocord or 2/0 nylon
Body:	Silver mylar
Tail or Rear Wing:	Four to ten white saddle hackles, with three to six strips of silver mylar on each side
Collar:	Red bucktail or calf tail
Topping:	Six to ten strands of peacock herl

TYING STEPS

1.   Place the hook in the vise and secure the thread at the bend. Then make several neat, contiguous wraps of thread to provide a friction base for tying on the hackle feathers.

2.   Choose white hackle feathers for the tail or rear wing. They should be uniform in color, size, shape, and texture. When installed, they should extend back one to two hook lengths beyond the bend. Usually four to ten feathers are used, with six being a good compromise for the average fly. The number will vary with the size of the fly and with the density of the fibers on the feathers. If possible, use straight feathers; however, if you must use those that are curved, choose them from opposite sides of the cape or saddle. When they're installed, be sure they curve downward.

3.   Prepare the feathers by stripping the fibers off the butt ends of the stems. Match up the tips and strip enough fibers off the base to make all feathers the same length. Be sure there is enough exposed stem to allow for secure tie-on; usually three-eighths or one-half inch is about right. When all feathers are precisely matched, strip a few more fibers off the bottom edge of the stems to aid in a smooth, even tie-on.

4.   Make the tail, or rear wing, in two separate halves, using half the feathers for each and matching them precisely in each assembly. Place the two assemblies together, dull-side to dull-side.

5.   Place a drop of cement on top of the hook at the point of tie-on and set the paired assemblies on top of the hook in proper position. The stems should be parallel to each other, *not* crossed, and centered on the shank.

6.   Hold the feathers firmly in place while tying them on. The first thread wrap should be just barely snug; in fact, depending on how many feathers are in the total, it may be necessary to make two or three wraps that are just snug. Too much pressure applied initially will almost undoubtedly torque the stems in the direction of the wrap, causing them to twist and rotate. After the first wrap or two, gradually tighten the thread for the next two or three wraps.

7.   Check the position and posture of the features. If satisfied, fix them in place with several neat wraps. Be sure to hold them securely, or they may still roll during the wrapping process. Apply cement to the tie-down area.

8.   Next, tie three to six narrow mylar strips, silver side out, on each side of the tail, securing them with several tight wraps. These strips are parallel to the hackle feathers and extend back about one-half of their length. I prefer mylar that is no more than ¹⁄₆₄-inch wide for this type of application, so that it retains its flexibility and flutter.

9.   Continue winding the thread forward in neat, contiguous wraps

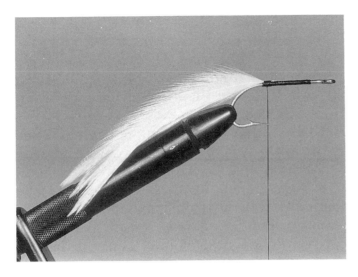

Tail secured in place.

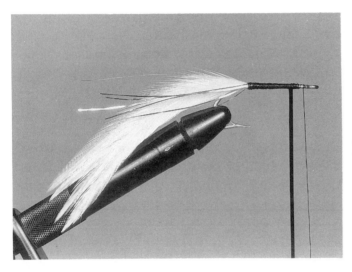

Narrow mylar strips on each side of tail. Wider mylar is tied in behind the eye for the body.

Mylar body completed.

to a point about one-quarter to three-eighths inch behind the eye. These wraps should be neat and contiguous to provide an even base for the mylar body. Tie in the mylar for the body and wind it back to the tail, then reverse it and wrap back to the point of original tie-on, securing it firmly in place. This is done exactly as it was for the Blonde, with the edge of the mylar on each wrap neatly abutting the previous wrap.

10.   The collar is next. Choose red bucktail long enough that the tips extend well beyond the point at which the mylar strips were tied on. They then merge with the tail or rear wing to retain the minnow-like configuration. The collar should be dense enough to be distributed quite fully around the entire circumference of the hook shank. It's usually easiest to tie the hair on in two separate bunches. At any rate, after cutting off the hair, preen and comb it as was done for the Blonde, then even the tips somewhat with a hair tamper.

11.   Secure the first bunch of hair on the bottom of the hook with several firm tight wraps. Be sure to work the hair halfway around the hook, so the entire bottom and lower half on each side are covered. If you don't have a rotating vise, check the far side with a small hand-held mirror. The hair can be tied on the bottom in either of two ways: Either leave the hook in the vise in the conventional manner and hold the hair under the hook as you wrap, or invert the hook in the vise for the tie-on procedure.

12.   Tie the second bunch of hair on top of the hook, again using several secure wraps, and work the hair around to distribute it halfway around the hook. Before going any further, make sure the hair is evenly distributed on each side, merging fully with the bunch tied on the bottom. If it's not, you may want to add a few hairs to either or both sides.

13.   After securing the last bunch of hair, build a fairly level surface over the tie-down area with the thread to accommodate the herl topping. If the herl is tied to a steeply tapered area, it will extend above the body of the fly in a continuation of that angle rather than follow the run of the hair.

14.   Bind the herl in place, starting at the front end of the level surface and working back, then forward. If the herl has a natural curve to it, make sure it points down, even if it's necessary to tie the strands on individually. Do not wind beyond the end of the level thread base or you will pull the herl down into the bucktail.

15.   Taper the head, whip-finish, and apply lacquer. The application of quick-drying epoxy or super glue after the lacquer has dried will greatly enhance the durability of the fly.

Bucktail collar secured in place and flowing back to merge with tail.

Herl topping tied in. The fly is complete.

RANDOM NOTES

The Deceiver is almost undoubtedly the most popular fly in salt water. As a result, it's tied in numerous colors. Several of those that are considered somewhat standard in solid colors are white, black, and yellow. Standard multicolor flies, with the color of the collar given first and the tail last, are blue and white, green and white, red and white, and red and yellow. An interesting innovation used by some tyers is to add a grizzly hackle feather to each side of the tail, giving a realistic barred effect. The fly is also tied with the lower portion of the collar the same color as the tail while the upper portion is of a contrasting color.

Topping may or may not be used. If it is, herl is normally chosen, but dyed bucktail is also used.

Another interesting option is the addition of eyes. The types of eyes used and the methods of applying them are almost as varied as the many colors used in the fly. Some fishermen feel the eyes do nothing more than dress up the fly; however, I'm convinced they add considerably to its productivity. If not, they certainly do no harm and, in most cases, are easy to apply, so why not take advantage of them?

The most common method of applying eyes has been to paint them on; however, some tyers glue doll eyes in place. A new method, gaining rapidly in popularity, is the use of lead eyes—they not only give the fly an optical appearance, but add a controlled amount of weight.

If eyes are to be painted on, the head is usually made oversize and an eye is placed on each side, usually yellow or white, with a black pupil. I prefer adding a shoulder of mallard, teal, or Amherst pheasant to each side and painting the eye on that. This method allows for realistic placement of the eye, and it can be made any size desired. Further, if Amherst pheasant is used, the black edge on the feather simulates the rear edge of a gill cover.

Doll eyes made of plastic are available in most craft stores and come in a variety of sizes and colors. Most have movable pupils. Doll eyes can be glued directly on the fly, or a monofilament stem can be glued to the back and the stem then secured to the hook.

Lead eyes are small, dumbbell-shaped pieces of lead alloy, and they're available in six different sizes, ranging in weight from $\frac{1}{100}$ to $\frac{1}{10}$ of an ounce. The enlarged area on each end is painted, and the connecting crossbar is then affixed to the hook. They're tied on just ahead of the collar, before finishing the head, and are secured with a series of tight figure-eight wraps. Before fixing the lead eyes to the fly, build a friction base on the hook shank with tying thread. Then hold the lead eyes in place with one hand while fastening them with a half-dozen or so figure-eight wraps. Before proceeding any further, place a drop of super glue on the winds and on the connecting bar portion of the lead eyes and let it dry. Next, take several clockwise wraps horizontally (in a plane parallel to the floor), *above the shank but beneath the lead eyes,* thus building a platform. Pull the thread in under the enlarged ends of the dumbbells so it's tight against the connecting bar. Finish off with several more figure-eight wraps, saturate the area with cement, and when that's dry, apply super glue again. The overall procedure is easy and takes much less time than the explanation. However, it must be emphasized that the numerous tight wraps and the separate applications of glue are essential to prevent the eyes from twisting or rotating on the hook shank during fishing.

One last item before leaving the Deceiver. The amount of material tied on at the bend can create considerable bulk, making it difficult to attain a nicely tapered body in that area. The problem can be avoided by

Lead eyes. A friction base is wound on the shank, and the lead eyes are held in place with a few figure-eight wraps and super glue.

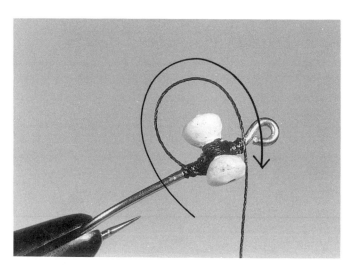

A platform of thread is built by wrapping the thread on a horizontal plane around the point at which the eyes are connected to the shank. The thread is wound under the eyes but above the shank, and is then pulled tight under the enlarged ends of the dumbbells.

The lead eyes are secured with additional tight figure-eight wraps and another application of super glue.

binding a piece of yarn to the top of the shank. The yarn acts as a filler or underbody and smooths out the transition from the hackle stems to the shank. The easiest time to apply the underbody is when working the thread forward in preparation for tying on the mylar for the body, in step 9. The thread does not have to be brought forward in contiguous wraps, but should be neat and wrapped closely enough to provide a smooth base for the mylar.

5

The Sea-Ducer

An advantage the previous two flies have in common is positive sink rate. Due to lack of resistance, they cut through the water readily, getting down to a working depth in a hurry provided they are adequately weighted or matched with a line of the proper density.

The Sea-Ducer, on the other hand, has exactly the opposite attribute. It sinks very slowly, and on a slow retrieve remains almost suspended at the depth at which the retrieve is started. This is due to a heavily hackled body that is palmer-wound. The fly looks like a mega-version of Hewitt's well-known dry fly, the Bivisible. As a result of its design, the Sea-Ducer is an exceptionally good choice for very shallow water. This doesn't mean it cannot be used in the deep—in fact, in large versions it's even used offshore. However, it was designed primarily as a shallow-water fly.

I don't know who created the pattern, but Eric Leiser states that well-known Miami fly tyer and angler Chico Fernandez is primarily responsible for its popularity and its name. Considering its seductive action in the water, it would certainly be difficult to come up with anything more appropriate than "Sea-Ducer."

I had fished similar but smaller versions of the same fly over a period of several years for largemouth bass, but used them only to a limited extent in the salt. It took one of Fernandez's articles to make me aware that the fly had all the attributes I was looking for in a pattern for fishing the mangroves for snook. The palmer-wound hackle on the Sea-Ducer buffers its entry into the water, minimizing the possibility of spooking the fish. In the water, the hackle slows the sink rate so it's not necessary to start stripping immediately, and a slow retrieve can be maintained. In addition, the soft palmered hackle responds to the slightest movement.

Fly-rodding for snook appeals to fishers from up north probably because of its similarity to bass fishing. Much of it consists of casting tight to shallow water cover without spooking the fish. In addition, the casts must often be right on the money time after time in order to trigger a fish into exploding under the lure.

And then the *real* challenge begins! I can assure you, after one session of coaxing snook out of the mangroves, you will either have lost every fish to the extensive underwater growth or you'll have subjected your tackle to stresses and strains you never dreamed it could withstand. The normal drill is for the fish to flash out of cover, swap ends as it takes the fly, and head right back for the maze of roots. It will pull like a mule, and if you don't apply maximum pressure it will gain the advantage. Usually, then, it's good-bye fish. On the other hand, if you're successful in holding it out for perhaps a minute or so, the fish will usually head for the sanctuary of deeper water. At that point, the fight is still far from over, but it does become somewhat more conventional.

I really admire snook—in my book they're a super fish. They're challenging, handsome, and exquisitely delicious on the table. Unfortunately, they're in trouble in many areas and should be harvested with the utmost discretion, and, of course, only in accordance with applicable gamefish laws.

The Sea-Ducer is productive on many other species of fish, and although I haven't tried it, I'm sure it would be very effective on channel bass. They often coexist with snook, and although they're not as spectacular, they're fun and do respond to a slowly retrieved fly.

A very popular color for snook in any type of lure is all-yellow or yellow with red trim, so let's fashion our first Sea-Ducer with a yellow tail, a body of yellow palmered hackle, and a red collar.

YELLOW-AND-RED SEA-DUCER

GENERAL DESCRIPTION

The Sea-Ducer is a minnow-like imitation. Several long hackle feathers are tied on at the bend and extend back to form the rear half of the fly. These feathers are installed shiny-side to shiny-side so they splay outward. Narrow strips of mylar, Krystal Flash, or other similar material are then added to each side of this tail, or rear-wing, section. The body consists of several saddle hackles that are palmered around the hook shank from the tail to a point a short distance from the eye of the hook. Usually the last one or two hackles installed, those immediately behind the eye, are of a contrasting color.

The location of the tail, or rear wing, at the bend adds length to the fly while decreasing the chance of its fouling around the gape. The palmer-wound body, as previously mentioned, affects the sink rate and provides sensitive breathing action with the slightest movement.

DRESSING AND COMPONENTS

Hook:	Mustad 3407 or 34007, #2 to 4/0
Thread:	Red, 3/0 Monocord or 2/0 nylon
Tail (Rear Wing):	Four to six yellow saddle hackles, with three to six narrow strips of silver mylar on each side
Body:	Four to six yellow saddle hackles palmered around shank
Collar:	One or two red saddle hackles, palmered at front end of body

TYING STEPS

1. Place the hook in the vise, secure the thread at the bend, and build a friction base with neat, contiguous wraps of thread, as was done for the Deceiver.

2. Choose the yellow hackle feathers for the tail. I normally use four for a #2 hook, and six for anything larger. They should be long enough so that when installed they extend back one and a half to two shank lengths beyond the bend. Inasmuch as these feathers are to splay outward, they do not have to be precisely matched, but they should be close enough in size and shape to present an aesthetically pleasing appearance. More importantly, they should be relatively supple, so that

they work in the water. If I have a choice, I prefer a slight but pronounced curve to accentuate this movement.

3.   Prepare the feathers, as was done for the previous fly, by stripping hackle fibers off the butt ends. Bear in mind that the same precision
is not required. Be sure to expose enough stem that it can be properly
secured to the hook, and then remove a few extra fibers from the bottom
edge for a smooth tie-on.

4.   Make the tail up in two separate assemblies, using half the feathers in each. Place the two assemblies together as you did for the Deceiver,
but for this pattern position them convex to convex, splaying outward.

5.   Place a drop of cement on top of the hook at the tie-on point. Set
the two assemblies in place on top of the hook, making sure the stems are
parallel to each other and centered on the hook.

6.   Hold the assemblies firmly in place and tie them on as was done
for the Deceiver. The first one or two wraps should be just snug enough
to hold the feathers in place without twisting the hackle stems, and then
the succeeding wraps can be gradually tightened to secure them.

7.   Check the position of the feathers, and when satisfied, secure
them with several more neat wraps. Be sure to hold them while making
these final wraps or they may twist or roll around the shank. Place a drop
of cement on the wraps.

8.   Tie three to six mylar strips on each side of the hackle feathers.
These are usually about three-fourths the length of the feathers and,
preferably, no more than 1/32-inch wide to provide maximum suppleness.

9.   The palmered body will start just ahead of the tail, and is wound
forward to a point a short distance behind the eye of the hook. Depending on the size of the fly, four to six yellow saddle hackles will be required.

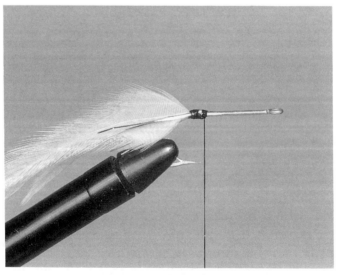

The tail, with mylar strips tied in.

Choose feathers that are wide enough so the hackle spread, when wound in place, will at least cover the gape of the hook. In addition, the feathers should have minimal taper so that the fibers, or barbules, on the usable portion are all close to the same length.

Note: Bear in mind that sharply tapered feathers will produce an abrupt taper when palmered onto the hook, due to the drastic difference in fiber length at each end of the feather. If it's necessary to use feathers with a substantial taper, strip barbules off the tip end until an appropriate fiber length is attained, and then tie the feather in by the tip. The fibers then get progressively longer, rather than shorter, as you approach the eye of the hook.

10.   Assuming hackle feathers with a gradual taper have been chosen, strip the unusable fibers off the butt ends, thus providing enough stem for a secure tie-on. Some tyers do a commendable job of securing all the feathers at once and winding them forward together, but I don't! When I try, it looks fine, but after I've secured everything and sit back to admire my work, I usually spot at least one hackle stem that is not tight to the shank. That leaves me two choices: Finish the fly, knowing it will eventually unravel, or take it apart and start over. I feel more comfortable working with one feather at a time as I wind them forward, and inasmuch as this produces a dense, durable body for me, that's the method I'll describe.

11.   Secure the butt end of one hackle stem to the underside of the hook with several tight wraps of thread. Grasp the hackle stem near the tip with the pliers and start winding it forward in closely spaced, but not touching, spirals. While winding the hackle, *be sure to keep the thread ahead of the stem* so it can be tied off. At this point, the wraps are *not* contiguous—

Hackle being palmer-wound. Note that the hackle is spiraled along the shank and the thread is kept ahead of the stem.

you should be able to see a small portion of the hook shank between each turn. You'll note that, because of the open spacing, none of the fibers have been wound down or trapped under preceding or succeeding turns. When the usable portion of the hackle has been wound in place, and before the barbules start to get noticeably shorter, switch the hackle pliers to your left hand (assuming you're a right-handed tyer). While maintaining tension on the end of the hackle feather, use your right thumb and index finger on the hook shank to compress the hackle turns tightly together. While doing this, you'll note that you gain some feather with your left hand, thus keeping the stem tight to the shank. Secure the hackle in place with several tight wraps immediately in front of the palmered hackle, and cut off the excess. The hackle turns are now contiguous and dense with a minimum of trapped barbules, resulting in a neat appearance.

12.   Tie the next hackle on immediately in front of the completed area and palmer it on in the same fashion. It will probably take three to five more hackles to complete the body; wind and compress each one as you continue forward. While working forward, bear in mind that the collar is going to require two to four turns of hackle, and the head will require additional space equivalent to about that same amount.

13.   Choose red hackle feathers the same approximate width as the body feathers, and prepare them in the same manner. Tie them to the underside of the hook, palmer them, secure them in place, and trim off the excess. Be sure to leave plenty of room for the head so it isn't crowded.

14.   Complete the head, whip-finish, and apply lacquer.

Hackle palmer-wound the length of the shank to form
body and collar.

COLOR OPTIONS AND ADDITIONAL NOTES

As with many saltwater flies, the multitude of color combinations are limited only by the tyer's imagination. In addition to the yellow and red, I've also found the following colors to be productive: yellow with either a blue or black collar; and white with a red, blue, or black collar.

My favorite, however, is to sandwich a grizzly hackle feather between two yellow or two white feathers when making up the tail assemblies. The dark bars of the grizzly show through the yellow or white of the cover feather when wet. I feel certain any of the above colors, in varying combinations and especially with the addition of grizzly to the tail, body, or both, will produce an effective fly.

One other option that should be considered is the addition of a weed guard. I've found the fly to be especially productive when fishing around heavy cover, and when casting close to decks and pilings during a strong tidal flow. Both situations result in numerous hang-ups—many of which can be avoided with an adequate guard. Needless to say, each hang-up can result in a lost fly, or worse, spoiling the water that's being fished.

There are several ways in which a hook can be made weedless. Following are two commonly accepted methods for installing a weed guard. One involves using twenty- or twenty-five-pound monofilament, while the other employs stainless-steel wire. I've found .014-inch diameter to be satisfactory for the wire. Both types are easy to install, as shown in the accompanying photos, and I've found them to be equally effective.

The completed fly. Note the tail feathers splaying
outward.

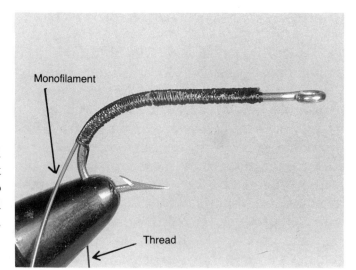

Monofilament weed guard. Monofilament is secured to the top of the shank and down into the bend.

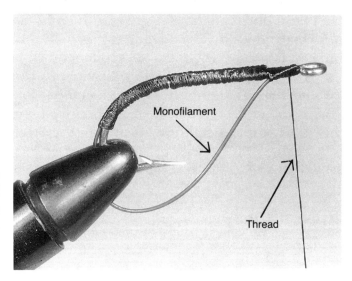

Monofilament is secured at the eye of the hook after the fly is completed.

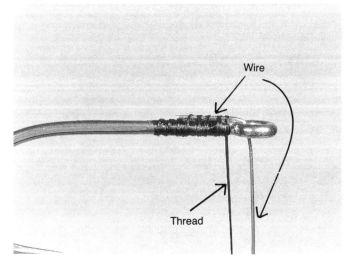

Wire weed guard. Wire is placed through the eye of the hook, bent down on top of the shank, and secured in place.

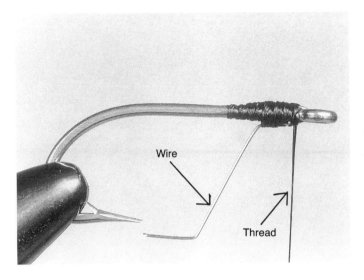

Wire is bent up under the shank and secured in place. It is then bent to shield the point of the hook.

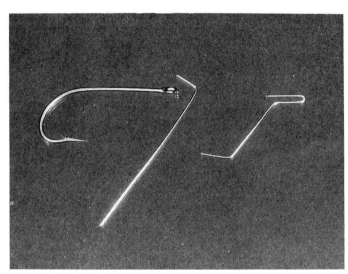

Middle, Wire as it is initially formed for securing to the top of the hook. *Right,* Wire in its completed shape.

6

The Glass Minnow

When I first saw the Glass Minnow many years ago, I considered it one of the cleverest innovations I'd seen in a long time. The body material was overwrapped with twenty- or twenty-five-pound monofilament, which not only protected the fragile body material but also gave it a fishy translucent appearance. According to Lefty Kreh, the practice of wrapping the body in this manner was first developed by Carl Hansen, and it has been popularized by Chico Fernandez. Although some referred to it as Glass Minnow, it was more popularly known at first as Monofilament Fly. Today the fly is often tied with an overwrap of one of the new clear-plastic materials such as Swannundaze or V-Rib, and it is customarily called a Glass Minnow.

At any rate, it's a fine all-purpose fly and is tied in a variety of sizes and colors. The wing is made of bucktail or calf tail and is almost always two separate colors. The lower portion is usually white, while the upper layer varies but is usually a darker, contrasting color. Inasmuch as one of the more common color combinations is green-over-white, let's tie our fly to match.

GREEN-OVER-WHITE GLASS MINNOW

GENERAL DESCRIPTION

As the name implies, the fly is a minnow pattern. The underbody is silver mylar with an overwrap of clear-plastic body material. The wing is tied on behind the eye of the hook and extends beyond the bend about one hook length. Depending on the size hook being used, the wing is made of bucktail or calf tail with a few strips of silver mylar tied on each side. Eyes are painted on either side of the head.

The fly casts well, is practically nonfouling, and because of the relatively sparse dressing, sinks well.

DRESSING AND COMPONENTS

Hook: Mustad 3407 or 34007, #6 to 3/0
Thread: Black 3/0 Monocord or 2/0 nylon
Body: Silver mylar with an overwrap of clear V-Rib
Wing: Bucktail in two layers, green over white, with three or
             four strips of silver mylar on each side
Eye: Painted yellow with black pupil

TYING STEPS

1.   Tie on behind the eye, wrap the thread smoothly to a point just shy of the bend, and fasten the V-Rib to the shank immediately aft of the contiguous thread wraps. Securing the V-Rib at that point and trimming the end of it in a long, angled cut will avoid an unsightly bump in that area.

2.   Allow the V-Rib to hang in a position that is out of the way, and wind the thread forward in close wraps, preparing a smooth foundation for the mylar. Secure the mylar to the shank about 3/16- to 1/4-inch behind the eye, allowing enough room to tie on the wing and complete the head.

3.   Coat the thread-wrapped shank with cement, then wind the mylar back to the V-Rib. Apply another coating of cement over the mylar and wind it forward over itself, securing it at the point of tie-on. The winds are made in neat contiguous wraps, as was done for the body of the Blonde.

4.   Apply another coat of cement over the completed mylar wrap, then wind the V-Rib forward in neat, adjacent turns, tying off where the mylar was secured. Prepare a smooth base for the wing with the thread.

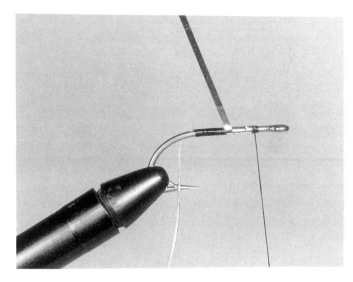

Mylar being wound.
Note the V-Rib tied
in at the bend.

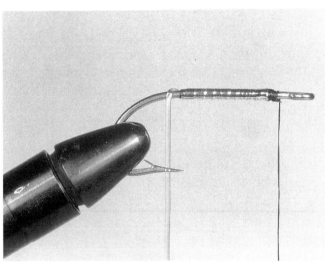

The mylar body
completed.

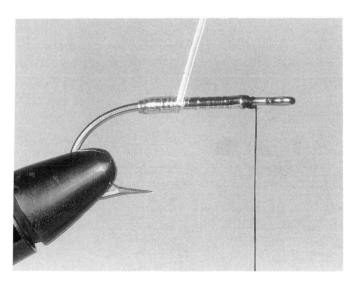

The V-Rib overwrap
being wound.

5. Cut and prepare two bunches of bucktail separately, one white and the other green. Each bunch should be half the diameter of a matchstick for a #1 hook, and about twice the length of the shank. For a larger or smaller hook, the diameter of the wing will be scaled up or down, but in any case should be relatively sparse. Prepare each bunch separately, combing, preening, and tamping to obtain the desired shape, as was done in preparing the wings for the Blonde.

6. Tie on each bunch separately, the white immediately over the shank and the green on top of that, applying a liberal coat of cement after each for increased durability. Bear in mind that the butt ends of the hair, after trimming, will be covered with thread and will help to form the tapered appearance of the completed head. Therefore, after tying on the white bunch, trim the forward end at an angle slanting down toward the eye of the hook. Wrap this slanted area with thread to provide the foundation for the forward portion of a neatly tapered head. Then, although the green bunch is to be the same length as the white, tie it in just behind the angled cut so that when it is trimmed, the same continuous taper is maintained through both the white and the green.

7. Tie three or four narrow strips of mylar on each side of the wing. These strips should be 1/32- or 1/64-inch wide for maximum flexibility, and about the same length as the wing.

8. Continue wrapping to form a neatly tapered head, whip-finish, and apply cement.

9. Paint an eye on each side of the head, using yellow for the iris and black for the pupil. After the paint has thoroughly dried, apply super glue or quick-drying epoxy to protect the eye and increase the overall durability of the fly.

ADDITIONAL NOTES

When painting an eye on a head that's relatively small, I normally use a regular finishing nail to apply the paint. Dip the head of the nail in yellow lacquer or model paint, touch it to a piece of paper to remove any excess, then place it on the appropriate spot on the head. After the iris portion has dried, paint the pupil on in a similar manner. I use the small end of the same nail for the pupil, having previously filed off the sharp point to create an appropriately sized flat spot.

Variations in this fly revolve primarily around the material used for the overwrap of the body and the color of the wing. Some tyers still cover the underbody with monofilament—it is durable and makes a nice appearance. However, many use materials such as Body Glass, Swannundaze, and V-Rib because of the ease with which they're applied. Green, blue, black, and brown are most commonly used for the top wing layer,

The first layer of the wing tied in.

The completed Glass Minnow: mylar strips and the top layer of the wing are tied in, and eyes are painted on the head.

with white used for the lower portion. Other variations include changing the color to match the local forage as closely as possible, and at the other extreme, tying the fly all-white. I have seen some flies that have been tied with three separate colors in the wing, with the uppermost layer darkest, the middle lighter, and the lowest white.

In any case, no matter what color or what type of overwrap is used, the Glass Minnow certainly has a great deal of eye appeal, both to fish and fishermen.

7

The Sand Eel

A fly fisher plying the inshore waters of the Northeast Coast would be hard-pressed to come up with a more consistently productive fly than a good sand eel imitation—especially in the early fall when the stripers and blues are fattening up for their migration to winter quarters.

Although commonly known as a sand eel or sand launce, the proper name of the fish is American sand lance. In spite of the common name and the appearance—elongated and round in cross section—it *is* a fish. In fact, it is an extremely abundant species and an important source of food in northern waters on both coasts. There are times when sand eels are so plentiful that large schools of foraging gamefish are enticed right up into the wash. When a school of marauding blues moves through the surf driving the sand eels ahead, the eels make a frenzied dash for the beach, where they strand themselves. They die in vast numbers, forming lengthy windrows along the sand. At times these windrows are nearly continuous and extend from several hundred feet to hundreds of yards long. If the blues sweep through a second or third time as the tide recedes, successive windrows are established, clearly marking the level of the tide at each foray. The always hungry sea gulls usually clean the rows in a hurry.

In addition to its numbers, there are two other attributes that make the sand eel especially attractive to the fly caster. First, directly related to its abundance is the fact that it's often available in vast numbers over shallow sandy bottoms. This attracts gamefish to the shallows where both the small-boat and the land-based angler have access to them. Second, the sand eel's slim profile makes it relatively easy to tie a realistic, castable imitation.

There are many sand eel patterns, some extremely productive. A few are nothing more than a hook with a lengthy tail of hair and a body formed by wrapping chenille around the shank. Others use mylar piping to cover the shank and to form an extension that protrudes beyond the bend; this extension in some patterns uses a trailer hook at the rear end. Another popular pattern looks very much like an elongated Deceiver. It's slimmer for its length than a typical Deceiver, and is tied with green or olive hackle feathers. However, my favorite is a personal innovation. It's a bucktail-type streamer, and is unique in comparison to other sand eel patterns in that lead eyes are secured to the shank a short distance behind the eye of the hook. The placement of this added weight causes the fly to dive toward the bottom during each pause in the retrieve. If heavy-enough lead eyes are used for the depth and current and the pause-strip action is properly timed, the fly kicks up a puff of sand as it bounces along. The heavier lead eyes make a fly more difficult to cast, but the faster sink rate and the accentuated jigging action can improve the situation when the fish are uncooperative. There are two reasons for the productivity of the fly: its appearance, and its action during the retrieve. Sand eels in attempting to escape predators are capable of burrowing head-first into the sand to a depth of four or five inches, and the diving action of the fly tends to simulate that activity.

I tie the fly with an olive-over-white wing, and normally use peacock herl for a topping.

THE SAND EEL

GENERAL DESCRIPTION

The fly is a streamer-type pattern. The body is mylar with an over-wrap of clear V-Rib, and the wing is composed of two layers of bucktail. The lower layer is white with a few strips of mylar on each side, and is tied on at the bend. It extends back two to two-and-one-half hook lengths. The upper wing is olive and is tied on about one-half inch behind the eye of the hook. It's secured in a position parallel to the shank and flows back immediately over the lower, or rear, wing, forming a slim, continuous profile. It extends back to the same point as the lower wing. Several strands of peacock herl are then tied on as a topping.

Olive chenille and lead eyes are both secured to the shank immediately forward of the upper wing. The chenille is then wrapped in figure eights around the lead eyes and around the shank to develop a realistic head-like configuration.

The slim profile and placement of the wings permits relatively easy casting and minimizes the possibility of fouling. The sparse dressing, in combination with the lead eyes, causes the fly to sink readily, while the lead eyes accentuate the diving, jigging action.

DRESSING AND COMPONENTS

Hook:	Mustad 34011 (stainless) long shank, #1 to 2/0
Thread:	White, 3/0 Monocord or 2/0 nylon
Body:	Pearlescent mylar with an overwrap of clear V-Rib
Lower (Rear) Wing:	White bucktail with three or four strips of pearlescent mylar on each side
Upper (Forward) Wing:	Olive bucktail
Topping:	Six to eight strands of peacock herl
Eyes:	Lead eyes, painted yellow with black pupil
Head:	Olive chenille

The rear wing is tied in, the mylar strips in place. V-Rib is tied in at the bend; the butt end of the wing is secured to the top of the shank.

TYING STEPS

1.   Secure the thread a short distance behind the eye, wind back to the bend, then tie on a bunch of white bucktail. The bucktail should be a little less than the diameter of a wooden match and should extend back two to two-and-one-half hook lengths. For a size 2/0 hook, the butt ends should extend forward to a point about one-half inch behind the eye of the hook to allow for the lead eyes and chenille head.

2.   While the thread is still at the bend, secure three or four narrow strips of pearlescent mylar to each side of the wing. These strips are slightly shorter than the wing itself.

3.   Before advancing the thread farther ahead, secure a length of V-Rib to the side of the shank at the bend—actually, at the juncture of the hair and shank. Tying on at that location will prevent an unsightly bump and assure a neat, smoothly tapered body.

4.   Bind the butt ends to the top of the shank, as was done for the Blonde, and saturate with head lacquer. The windings do not have to be contiguous, but should be spaced closely enough to establish a smooth base for the mylar.

5.   Tie the pearlescent mylar on, wind it back to the bend, then forward over itself, securing it at the point at which it was tied on.

6.   Bring the V-Rib forward over the mylar in neat, contiguous wraps and secure it in place.

7.   The lead eyes, which should be painted beforehand, are secured in the space between the eye of the hook and the body, using the same method that was used for the Deceiver. Leave the thread positioned behind the lead eyes for the next procedure.

Note: For a 2/0 hook, the crossbar of the lead eyes should be about ⅜-inch behind the eye of the hook.

8.   Tie on a length of olive chenille between the lead eyes and the body.

9.   Wrap the chenille around the shank between the body and the lead eyes. Using both chenille and thread, build a base or platform for the upper wing. This base should be built up to the same height as the body—if it is lower, the thread will pull the butt ends of the bucktail down into the crevice, causing the wing to cock upward rather than lie parallel to the shank.

10.   Secure the upper wing over the base. This wing should be about the same diameter as the lower wing and extend back to the same point.

11.   Tie six to eight strands of peacock herl on top of the wing. The herl should extend back the same distance as the wing, and if any of it is naturally curved, make sure it points down.

Mylar is wound.

The V-Rib overwrap is complete. Lead eyes are installed, leaving room to complete either a chenille or ram's-wool head.

A chenille platform is built to provide a base for the forward wing.

The forward wing and topping are installed.

A completed Sand Eel with chenille head.

A Sand Eel with a ram's-wool head, prior to trimming.

12.   Wrap the chenille over the thread that secures the topping in place, figure-eight it around the lead eyes to form the head, then taper it neatly down to the eye of the hook.

13.   Secure the chenille, whip-finish, and apply lacquer to the thread.

OPTIONS

There are just a few options I apply to this particular fly, none of which drastically alter its appearance. They are: varying the size of the lead eyes; using silver in place of pearlescent mylar; substituting FisHair for both the bucktail and herl; and using olive ram's wool in lieu of chenille. I also use glass eyes at times, rather than the lead. They add more realism to the fly and are easier to cast; however, they do minimize the diving/jigging action during the retrieve. As to the lead eyes, I normally use those that weigh $\frac{1}{36}$ or $\frac{1}{24}$ ounce, but sometimes resort to heavier ones for use in deeper water, heavy currents, and strong tidal rips.

I'm partial to pearlescent mylar when fishing the gin-clear waters of the tropics, but for northern waters I probably tie fifty percent of my flies with silver mylar because of the additional flash.

Inasmuch as it is more durable than natural hair, I often use FisHair for bluefish flies. In this particular pattern I use the moss green color in place of the olive, and substitute black for the herl.

The ram's wool takes a little longer to apply than the chenille, but it makes a neater-looking head. Once the wool is wet, it aids in the sinking of the fly. If you haven't worked with it, try it—you'll like it! Tie the wool on in a manner similar to that used for deer body hair. It may not spin as easily as the deer hair; however, if necessary, just turn the hook over and add a bunch to the bottom. Continue adding bunches and packing them tightly together, whip-finish, and then trim to the desired shape.

The finished Sand Eel with a trimmed ram's-wool head.

One other note for those who haven't worked with pearlescent my-lar and V-Rib as body materials. The color of the body can be changed substantially or moderately by using colored thread as an initial wrap under the mylar. The color shows through, although somewhat altered by the pearlescent mylar, and produces a nice effect. It's worth experimenting with.

Wouldn't it be nice if colors, sizes, and terminology were standard throughout the tying industry? Especially for those of us who must mail-order most of our materials. For example, FisHair's moss green is the same color as, or is close to, the olive bucktail I've just obtained from two different, well-known sources. And this difference is minor compared to the inconsistencies in the line, hook, and tackle-manufacturing industries. Maybe someday!

THE SURF CANDY SAND EEL PATTERN—AND MORE

The fly we're about to discuss is another personal favorite. I was first introduced to its unique construction by Bob Popovics of Seaside Park, New Jersey. Bob is a superb fly tyer and fisherman, and, in my opinion, is one of the most innovative tyers on the saltwater scene today.

The fly, which was originally called the Surf Candy, is actually a style or design rather than a specific pattern. By using one basic technique and varying color, size, and body configuration, many species of forage fish can be imitated. In fact, Bob now ties a series of realistic flies that are collectively known as Pop-Fleyes.

Bob started out with the intention of developing a streamer-type fly that would be nonfouling when used in the surf. He not only accomplished that goal, but in so doing developed a fly that has an appealing translucent appearance, sinks readily without being difficult to cast, and is durable. What's more, it is easy to tie.

The major ingredient of the fly other than the basic tying materials is quick-drying epoxy. It is used to encapsulate the forward portion of the fly from the eye of the hook to the bend. A short-shank hook, such as Eagle Claw 254 SS, is normally used, in sizes 1 to 2/0. The wing is made of bucktail or synthetic material such as FisHair or Ultra Hair. It is tied in behind the eye of the hook just as it is for a conventional hairwing streamer. The wing is usually two or three different colors, and a small amount of hair is allowed to work around to the bottom of the shank to form a sparse underwing. A dark topping of herl or black hair may be applied.

Here is the technique that separates Bob's creation from the run-of-the-mill hairwing design. Mix up a small bunch of epoxy, perhaps the size

The finished Surf Candy.

Close-up of the head area on a Surf Candy.

of a quarter. Using a dubbing needle, apply it generously to the forward portion of the fly. Don't worry—you are not going to ruin a beautifully tied creation! In fact, you'll be pleased with the final results. A caution: Use something clean and nonabsorbent, such as a dubbing needle, to apply the epoxy. Some applicators, such as toothpicks and popsicle sticks, apparently contain resins or processing chemicals that are extracted from the wood by the epoxy, causing the coating to discolor within a matter of hours or days after curing.

Apply the epoxy to the top, bottom, and both sides of the fly, from the eye of the hook to the bend. The epoxy is relatively heavy and will tend to flow to the bottom of the hook. To distribute the epoxy evenly and avoid the formation of an unsightly glob at the bottom, remove the fly from the vise to apply it. Control the flow by rotating the fly and orienting it in different positions for the first two or three minutes after application. While the epoxy is setting up, you may want to pull on the hairs slightly to align them properly. As soon as the glue sets up, the fly can be placed back in the vise to complete curing.

It may be necessary to apply a second or third light coat to obtain a smooth finish. However, once you've tied a few Surf Candys, you'll produce a presentable-looking fly with the initial coat.

If a prism eye, painted eye, or other marking is to be applied to the forward portion of the fly, it is a good idea to think in terms of a second coat. Apply the markings after the first coat; the second coat, lightly applied, will provide a protective envelope over them while enhancing the finish.

I've often tied a sand eel pattern, using Bob's encapsulating technique, with a herl-over-olive-over-white wing, and have found it to be very productive. However, Bob often carries his designs much further. In addition to adding eyes, he uses a fine-point permanent marker to draw gills, mouth, and other appropriate markings. And for some patterns, he adds a cheek feather for gill covers.

He also installs a realistic tail on many of his flies by cutting two matching hackle feathers to the appropriate shape and then gluing them together dull-side to dull-side. The stems of the feather assembly are tied to a short length of straight monofilament. The monofilament is passed through a short length of braided mylar tubing and the entire assembly is secured to the top of the hook. Another piece of braided mylar is then wound over the tie-down area to cover the thread. The feathers, of course, form the tail, and the braided mylar gives a scale-like, sparkly appearance to the longitudinal axis of the fly.

Using these techniques, Bob ties extremely realistic versions of spearing, mullet, rainfish, menhaden (bunker), and other forage fish common to the mid-Atlantic Coast. Using these same techniques, along with your imagination, you can easily duplicate the forage in your area.

The Surf Candy with
a tail.

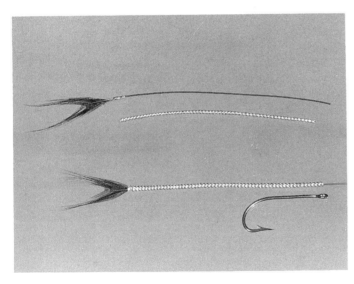

The tail assembly for
a Surf Candy.

8

Squid Patterns

The squid, or calamary, fills a special niche in the ecology of the sea. A relentless predator, it is also heavily preyed on by the vast majority of gamefish. In fact, it is often the major source of food for some species of fish.

There are several hundred species of squid, and they range in size from a fraction of an inch to several feet long. Some live at the surface, while others exist at varying depths to as much as a mile below the surface. Some even "fly" quite regularly, and it's not uncommon for one to land on the deck of a boat. Because of the substantial variations in size and habitat, squid are available as prey to most pelagic and bottom-dwelling fish.

Squid are one of the most widely imitated of all saltwater forage, and whole and cut squid are used as bait throughout the world. The artificials are usually made of feathers or plastic and are used for trolling. Although we tend to think of them as only a saltwater lure, the small plastic imitations are fast approaching a zenith in popularity for Pacific salmon in the Great Lakes.

The squid is unique in appearance and action as compared to most of the fish-foods tyers imitate. As a result, there are a few characteristics I

feel are essential in a good imitation. Squid swim by jet propulsion and can move rapidly in either direction, but they normally swim backwards: The tapered end, which contains two lateral fins, cuts through the water while the arms trail behind. This is the configuration in which all squid imitations are made. Squid have very pronounced and highly visible eyes and ten arms, two of which are tentacles. They are masters at camouflage and can change pattern and color rapidly. They are capable of changing from an almost colorless translucency to various shades of blue, red, purple, yellow, brown, and many hues in between. I once had one land alongside me on the thwart of a small boat off Cape Cod, and I sat in absolute amazement as it went back and forth through its entire repertoire of color changes in an unsuccessful effort to blend with the gray surface on which I sat.

There are two squid patterns that I favor, each being substantially different than the other. One is tied with feathers and chenille, and the other is made from deer hair and rubber hackle. Both flies are constructed to swim in the conventional manner, and each has eight to ten arms, giving the fly a full appearance and an enticing, wriggly action. Each pattern has highly pronounced eyes.

Both are intended primarily for casting; however, they are also very effective trolling lures. When fishing either of the flies, and whether casting or trolling, I tend to move the fly in occasional spurts to simulate the jet-propelled action of the real thing.

THE SHADY LADY SQUID

The feather pattern is called the Shady Lady Squid, and it is another of Bob Popovics's innovations. It's a pattern that clearly illustrates Bob's tying skills.

GENERAL DESCRIPTION

This fly is a lifelike representation of a squid, with long saddle hackles for arms and a body formed by winding Poly Flash, a chenille-like material, around the shank. Glass eyes are located on the shank a short distance forward of the bend, and the body is tapered down toward the eye of the hook.

Although the fly is relatively large, it casts quite well and is practically nonfouling, due to the placement of the arms at the bend.

DRESSING AND COMPONENTS

Hook: Mustad 3407 or 34007, 3/0 to 5/0
Thread: White or matching color, 3/0 Monocord or 2/0 nylon
Arms: Eight to ten long white saddle hackles, along with a dozen or so strips of pearlescent Krystal Flash
Body: White Poly Flash
Collar: White hackle, palmer-wound
Eyes: Glass with wire attached, 6 to 8 mm, clear or amber with black pupil

Note: The forward portion of the body, from the collar to the eye of the hook, is given two or three heavy coatings of clear quick-drying epoxy to form a smooth, durable body. The epoxy allows the underbody material to show through and gives it an appealing, translucent appearance.

TYING STEPS

1. Secure thread at the bend and, using chenille, build a bump about ⅛-inch in diameter around the hook shank. This will aid in keeping the saddle-hackle arms spread apart.

2. Select eight to ten saddle hackles, about 3½ to 4 inches long for a 5/0 hook. The number chosen will vary according to their width, the object being to cover the hook shank around its periphery. Prepare the saddles for tie-in by stripping the butt ends. Leave some of the fluffy material on, because it tends to effect a skirtlike appearance around the base of the arms when secured in place. Tie them on immediately forward of the chenille bump, securing them two or three at a time to insure distribution around the hook shank.

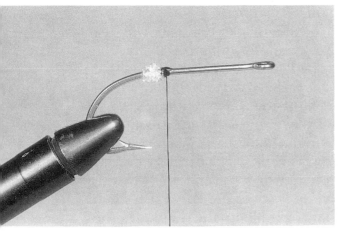

The chenille bump.

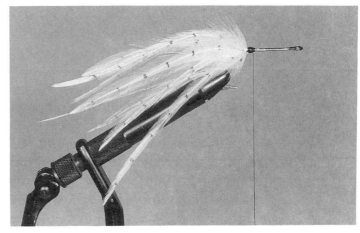

The feather arms are tied in.

Krystal Flash is secured alongside the arms, and the Poly Flash "chenille" is tied in.

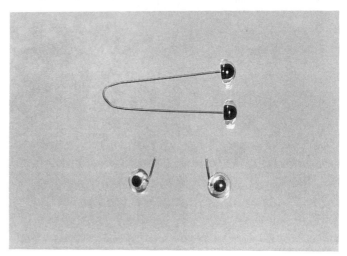

A close-up of the glass eyes. The lower pair are prepared for tie-in.

3. Secure the Krystal Flash in place so that it extends back with the arms and is distributed around the shank.

4. Tie white Poly Flash to the hook shank over the tie-down area and take several turns to cover an area, laterally along the shank, the width of the glass eyes. The eyes will be tied on next, so bear in mind that the Poly Flash will show through the transparent iris. Place the excess material in a clip or allow it to hang in an out-of-the-way position.

5. Cut the wire stem on each glass eye so that it's approximately half an inch long. Lay the stem parallel to the hook shank just forward of the Poly Flash, with the eye extending back over it. Next, bend the eye out at a right angle so the wire stem has a ninety-degree bend in it where it meets the hook shank. Position the eye so it's over the Poly Flash, then bind down the portion of the stem that is parallel to the shank. Do the same for the other eye, and then cement the area thoroughly, covering the two wire stems and windings along their entire lengths.

Glass eyes are secured in place, and Poly Flash is wound just forward of the eyes.

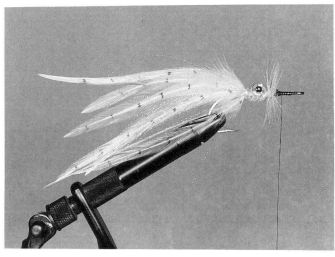

The palmer-wound collar.

6.   Figure-eight the Poly Flash around the shank and the stems of the eyes to properly fill the area, then tie off.

7.   Tie in a white saddle hackle by the butt end immediately forward of the glass eyes, and take three or four turns of hackle around the shank, forming a palmer-wound collar.

8.   A round tapered toothpick is used on each side of the hook shank as a filler to provide the body with some width while maintaining a slim profile when viewed from the side. Cut the toothpick to the proper length so that it extends from the collar to just behind the eye of the hook. Bind one to each side of the hook with the narrow end forward. Finish with the thread back at the collar.

9.   Tie the Poly Flash back in just forward of the collar and wind it forward over the hook shank and the toothpick fillers in neat, contiguous wraps. Tie it off and whip-finish.

10.   To complete the fly, two or three epoxy coatings are applied.

Toothpicks are lashed to each side of the shank.

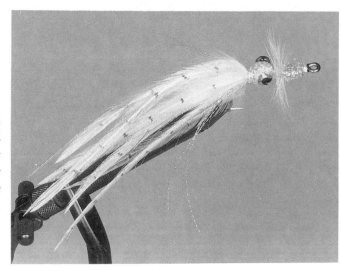

Poly Flash is tied in again and wound forward to cover the toothpicks and the remainder of the shank.

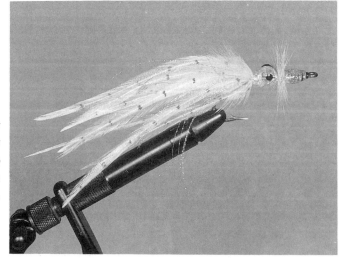

The finished Shady Lady Squid. Epoxy has been applied to the forward portion of the fly.

Using quick-drying or five-minute epoxy, apply a fairly heavy coat directly over the Poly Flash from the hackle collar to the eye of the hook. Some of the epoxy will work down into the material, but epoxy is heavy and will tend to run to the bottom of the hook, creating an unsightly glob. To counteract this, take the fly out of the vise while applying the epoxy. Keep rotating it and moving it around to control the flow for the first two or three minutes, as was done for the Surf Candy. Once the epoxy stops flowing, the fly can be placed back in the vise to complete curing. The fly may have a rough, unkempt appearance—actually, messy is a better word—after the first coat. However, the second coat, applied in the same manner and rotated as it dries, will fill in around it and smooth it out. If the appearance still leaves something to be desired, don't hesitate to apply a third coat.

Close-up of the area covered with epoxy.

VARIATIONS

Bob Popovics ties this fly in many colors, including white, orange, green, pink, and red. He substitutes mylar or Flashabou for the Krystal Flash, and often uses Spectra Chenille, rather than palmer-wound hackle, to form the collar. In addition, using a fine-point felt-tip marker, he often adds markings to the saddle-hackle arms to provide a mottled appearance. These are added randomly and are short "dashes," about 1/16-inch long, that run across the feather. Going down the length of the feather, they will be more or less parallel to one another and spaced 1/2- to 3/4-inch apart. Bob uses colors that are somewhat akin to the basic color of the feather, rather than drastic contrasts. For example, red may be used on orange, or perhaps dark green on a light green feather. Bob also ties this fly much larger, including some of sufficient size for offshore fishing. The larger versions are tied by using heavy monofilament (forty- or fifty-pound test) as an extension of the hook shank. In such cases, the mono-filament is strung between two vises and a friction base is built up on it to provide a proper surface to which the fly-tying materials can be affixed. Almost the entire fly is secured to the monofilament, including the eyes and the collar. The epoxied body is then formed, using the entire length of the hook shank.

DEER-HAIR SQUID

I use at least two colors to give this fly a varied or blotchy ap-pearance, and am partial to white with a patch of purple on each side. These were the colors that predominated during most of the color changes I observed in my encounter off Cape Cod, and they remain my favorite. I've taken more fish on that color combination than any other, but I'm sure that's due to the fact that I use it the most. But I have confidence in it, and anyone who has spent much time pursuing gamefish with artificials knows that confidence is essential to consistent success.

GENERAL DESCRIPTION

The fly has a squidlike configuration employing rubber hackle for the arms and deer hair for the body. The arms are tied in at the bend, and the hair is spun on the remainder of the shank. While building the deer-hair body, lead eyes, glass eyes, or bead-chain eyes are positioned along the shank to simulate prominent, realistic eyes. The deer-hair body is then trimmed to the proper shape, with lateral fins on each side. The placement of the arms, along with the material from which they're made, make the fly nonfouling. The rubber bands shimmy and undu-late constantly, adding substantially to the fly's ability to entice a strike.

DRESSING AND COMPONENTS

Hook: Mustad 34011, long shank, 1/0 to 4/0
Thread: White, 3/0 Monocord or 2/0 nylon
Arms: Ten strips of white rubber hackle, approximately ³⁄₃₂-inch wide
Body: Deer body hair, white and purple
Eyes: Bead-chain, glass, or lead eyes, yellow with black pupil

TYING STEPS

1.   Tie in near the bend, build a friction base of thread, and secure the rubber-hackle arms in place. I tie these on three or four at a time, making sure they're distributed evenly around the hook. The arms are about 2½ inches long for a 2/0 hook.

2.   Cut a bunch of white body hair about ¼-inch in diameter, comb out the underfur, and spin the body hair onto the shank immediately forward of the area in which the arms are tied on. The tips of the hair should point back toward the bend so they form a mantle or skirt over the base of the arms. I usually add a small bunch of a contrasting color—in this case purple—to each side so that color extends back into the skirt. Using heavy-duty scissors, give the butt ends of the hair a rough trimming—not a final trim, but enough so they don't interfere with the next step.

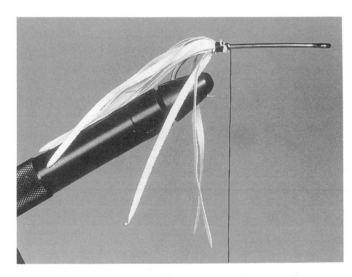

Rubber hackle arms are tied in.

The deer-hair skirt.

3.   Build another friction base with the thread and firmly secure the eyes in place. On a 2/0 hook, I use eyes that are about ⁶⁄₃₂- to ⁷⁄₃₂-inch in diameter. In the lead eyes, that is the ½₄-ounce size. They should be painted beforehand. In glass eyes, I use those that are 3 to 6 mm in diameter.

4.   Immediately in front of the eyes, continue spinning and packing bunches of deer hair to a point just behind the eye of the hook, leaving enough room to properly finish the head of the fly.

5.   After tying all that hair on, it's necessary to cut most of it off to shape the fly properly. I've seen some tyers who are very adept at trimming with a razor blade; however, I do a much better job and feel more comfortable with scissors. First, I shape the profile as viewed from the side. In shaping the top, I start at the eye of the hook and trim back toward the skirt—the body tapers up very slightly from the forward end back toward the eyes. It then levels off just above the eyes and is trimmed back to the skirt. The bottom is shaped in a similar manner, but is trimmed much closer to the shank to insure that interference in the gape of the hook is minimal.

The butt ends of the skirt are trimmed, and lead eyes are installed.

Deer hair is spun the entire length of the shank.

Initial trimming. The fly's profile as viewed from the side.

Initial trimming. A top view of the trimmed fly.

6.   The next step is to shape the fly as viewed from the top. It's from this angle that the lateral fins are apparent. There is one on each side, and although they are located at the tail end of the squid, they are at the front end of the fly. (Remember, the squid swims backward.) First, trim each side parallel to the hook shank, working forward from the skirt to the position at which the fins are to start. This portion of the squid's body is the same width or slightly narrower than the width of the glass, lead or bead-chain eyes.

7.   The fins are about one-third the length of the hook shank, and each one is triangular in shape, with the apex of the triangle projecting out from the body about one-half of the body's width. In shaping the fins, I start just behind the eye of the hook, trim out to the apex, then trim back to the point at which the fin meets the body.

Second trimming. The sides of the body are trimmed to leave enough deer hair for fins.

Final trim. The fins are formed.

The finished Deer-Hair Squid.

8. The outline of the body as viewed from both the top and the side is now ready for final shaping. The final trim consists merely of rounding off the body, then trimming the fins to the appropriate thickness by cutting hair from both the top and the bottom. After the fins are trimmed to the desired thickness, I saturate them with head lacquer, then squeeze the hair together with my fingers to stiffen them and make them tougher.

9. Complete the fly with a whip-finish, and apply cement to the head. Then, using the dubbing needle, work a liberal amount of cement into the belly of the fly to increase its durability.

VARIATIONS

I vary the color a great deal, running the entire range of shades available and always using at least two colors per fly to maintain the blotchy appearance. The size of the eyes will vary with the size of the fly and the desired sink rate. If the fly is to be fished on top or in the surface film, I use bead chain, while for a sinking model I use either glass or lead eyes. No matter what size eyes are installed, you'll probably have to resort to a sink-tip or full-sinking line to get the fly down, at least until it becomes thoroughly saturated.

One suggestion on the material used for the arms. I prefer rubber wiggle skirts, such as those used on spinning and plug-casting lures, over conventional rubber hackle. The wiggle skirts are more expensive, but you can tie several squid from one skirt, and the individual strands do not have a tendency to split lengthwise, as the rubber hackle sometimes does.

TIPS ON SPINNING DEER HAIR

Spinning deer hair seems to be a bugaboo for many tyers. Strangely, although I may have some difficulty with other tying disciplines, spinning hair seems to be my forte. I suppose it's because my tying career started in a somewhat backward sequence: I tied practically nothing but bass bugs for years before branching out into other fly types. Here are some tying suggestions that I feel are very helpful in constructing a high-quality deer-hair fly. If spinning hair is the bane of your existence, it may be helpful to consider these as practice exercises.

1. **Spinning.** Cut a bit of hair about ¼-inch in diameter. This amount will vary with your skill and what you want to accomplish. However, too large a bunch is difficult to handle and may eventually work loose. Too small a bunch means that many more bunches are

needed to fill a given space, which, in turn, means more wraps of thread.

Hold the bunch on top of the hook parallel to the shank, and take two turns of thread around the bunch and the hook. Apply pressure by pulling down on the thread, and as it starts to flare, slowly release the bunch. At the same time, while applying constant pressure with the thread, take two or three more turns through the flaring hair, following the same path with the thread. These additional turns will create torque on the bunch and cause the hair to work around the shank. Advance the thread through the hair to the bare wire, take one more turn around the shank, and apply a half-hitch.

2. **Spotting.** This is actually another method of spinning hair; however, I like to refer to it as "spotting" because with subtle changes in technique a tyer can cause the hair to spin all the way around the shank, or "spot" it, at any point around the circumference of the wire.

It does take practice and depends on two functions. First, it is necessary to develop a feel for when to release finger pressure on the hair, and to release that pressure in a controlled manner as the hair flares. Second, and this is especially important if you want to spot the hair, pressure from the thread must be applied directly opposite the point at which the hair is to remain. For example, if you want the hair to stay directly on top of the hook, pull straight down. The normal tendency when bringing the thread around to the bottom of the hook is to go beyond the vertical and pull the thread back toward oneself. This creates torque on the bunch of hair and rotates the bunch to the opposite side of the hook or around to the bottom.

When spotting the hair, start out just as was done for spinning, but after it starts to flare do not take additional turns through it because they will create torque and undo what has just been accomplished. Instead, with the hair positioned where you want it, hold it in place while advancing the thread forward, then finish off as was done in spinning.

3. **Stacking.** This is a technique in which two or more different colors are placed in the same position, laterally, along the shank one on top of the other. Start spinning hair of the first color to be used in the conventional manner. As it starts to flare, apply the torquing technique, bringing the hair around to the bottom of the shank. Take one or two more turns through the hair, holding the bunch in place if necessary. Don't advance the thread, but allow the weight of the bobbin to maintain tension.

Prepare another bunch of hair of the second color, and place it over the first bunch. Take two turns, following the same path, and pull straight down to spot the hair on the top half of the shank. Take two more turns to further secure it. If a third color is to be added, don't advance the thread.

To add the third color, cut a bunch a bit smaller in diameter than the first two. Using your finger, make an indentation in the top of the body where you want to place the third color. Hold the bunch down in the indentation, spot it in place with two turns of thread, then advance the thread forward to the bare wire.

4. **Retaining tips of hair.** This technique is useful where it is desirable to retain the tips of the hair to form a tail, wing, or skirt, such as in the squid imitation. It also makes it easier to trim the butt ends without inadvertently cutting the tips.

When spinning hair in the conventional way, the thread is passed over the center of the bunch. When the hair flares, both the butt and tip ends are the same length, causing them to intermix. In order to keep them separated, pass the thread over the bunch closer to the butt ends. When the hair flares, the butt ends will be much shorter than the tips and can easily be trimmed by pushing the tips out of the way with the back of the scissors blade. The length of the tip ends is controlled by the spot over which the thread is passed.

5. **Increasing durability.** This method of increasing the life of the fly also enhances its floating qualities by making the body more dense. Spin the hair in the conventional manner, but after every second or third bunch pack the hair especially tight, apply three or four extra half-hitches, then cement.

9

Tarpon Flies

I want to emphasize that the title of this chapter is meant in the generic sense only. I don't want to imply that these are the only flies capable of taking tarpon any more than I want to give the impression that they are productive for tarpon only and will take nothing else. The flies we're about to discuss are effective on many species of fish, just as there are other patterns that are very productive on tarpon.

We will be tying two very different styles, almost opposites in design and use. The common denominator in each is that both are used extensively for tarpon and are very productive when used as intended.

One style is used primarily in shallow water, especially on the gin-clear flats of the tropics. The flies in this genre are often referred to as shallow-water, keys-, or flats-type tarpon flies. Some have very specific names, others do not, but all use the same basic design. They are lightly dressed so they cast relatively well, and because they're tied with splayed-out wings and a few turns of palmer-wound hackle, they're animated by the slightest rod movement.

The other style is heavily dressed and is intended for use where a highly visible fly is desired. It's commonly used in deep or murky water and in tidal rips and heavy currents where water action tends to compress the fly. In addition, bead chain is installed behind the eye of the hook, and it is generally accepted that this, along with the heavy dressing, tends to set up vibrations and impulses as water moves over and around the fly. This, in turn, increases the probability of the fly being detected under conditions of poor visibility. This design is undoubtedly the most popular fly on the east coast of Costa Rica, where heavy currents often prevail. The bulky dressing is supple and resilient; consequently, these flies are easily animated. The slightest rod movement causes them to breath, and even when hanging still in heavy currents the materials tend to work almost constantly as the water flows over them. They're tied in a multitude of colors and with many personal innovations, and are often weighted or fished with a fast-sinking line, quite often lead-core. As with the shallow-water flies, these are also referred to in terms of the habitat in which they're used: i.e., deep-water flies, or Costa Rica tarpon flies.

Although tarpon are extremely aggressive when hooked, they commonly respond to a very slow retrieve. Because of this, the breathing action of the flies and the slight stimulus required to animate them is a big plus.

An even more bewildering aspect of tarpon behavior is the size of the lure they'll move to. I'm always amazed when I see a tarpon of perhaps eighty pounds or more rocketing into the air with a three- or four-inch fly in its mouth. It certainly makes the old adage, "a big bait for a big fish" look like Swiss cheese.

The fight of a tarpon is spectacular, and although these fish are capable of graceful greyhounding leaps, they usually launch themselves with what appears to be a violent, uncontrolled explosion triggered by absolute panic. Fortunately for the angler, the vast majority of tarpon jump repeatedly, which tires them in relatively short order. Even at that, it's often necessary to up-anchor and follow a good-sized fish a substantial distance before it's landed. Fish that decide to run, rather than jump, might never be landed unless the angler has the ability to follow. Even with that ability, and a fish that tires itself by jumping frequently, it's common for a fight with a very large fish to last several hours.

The tarpon has many names, both complimentary and otherwise, and several of these range from uncomplimentary to unprintable. However, one name that certainly fits and wears very well is the Silver King.

The flies in this chapter are effective in their intended environments and relatively easy to tie.

Argentine Blonde
Deceiver

Sand Eel
Sea-Ducer   Glass Minnow

Deer-Hair Squid
Shady Lady Squid

TARPON FLIES
Deep Water
Shallow Water

BONEFISH FLIES
Crazy Charlie Brown
Bonefish Special   Horror

PERMIT FLIES
Pink Shrimp
Puff   Deer-Hair Crab

Barracuda Fly
Trolling or Tandem Fly

Epoxy Fly (Rotated)   Free-Body or Flexible Slider
Epoxy Fly (Molded)   Fixed-Body Popper

THE SHALLOW-WATER TARPON FLY

This fly was originated many years ago by Stu Apte, well-known Florida angler and guide and holder of several saltwater fly-rod records. The fly is tied with yellow and orange saddle hackles.

GENERAL DESCRIPTION

The fly is tied with all of the materials at the bend of the hook, and the remainder of the shank is either bare or covered with nothing more than thread or paint. The completed fly looks very much like an unfinished version of one previously tied, the Sea-Ducer. The tail, or rear wing, consists of six to eight hackle feathers tied to splay outward. The orange feathers are innermost on each side, while the yellow is tied in on the outboard side of the orange. Immediately forward of the tail, a collar is formed with yellow-and-orange-mixed saddle hackles, palmer-wound for a total of two to six turns. The remainder of the shank may be left completely exposed, or it may be covered with orange or red thread.

This fly, for all practical purposes, is nonfouling due to the location of the materials at the rear end of the shank, a very desirable attribute on the windy flats where it's most often used.

DRESSING AND COMPONENTS

Hook:	Mustad 3407 or 34007, #2 to 5/0
Thread:	Red or orange, 3/0 Monocord or 2/0 nylon
Tail (Rear Wing):	Two bright orange saddle hackles, with four or six yellow saddle hackles
Collar:	One bright orange and one yellow saddle hackle
Body (Hook Shank):	Left bare or covered with tying thread to a point a short distance behind the eye

TYING STEPS

1. Place the hook in the vise, secure the thread at the bend, and build a friction base, as was done for the Sea-Ducer.
2. Select the yellow and orange saddle hackles for the tail. Two of each color are used by some tyers no matter what size hook is used, but

most use two orange and four to six yellow. The feathers should be long enough to extend beyond the bend about two shank lengths.

3.   Prepare the feathers as was done for the Sea-Ducer, then make up two tail assemblies. These assembles will splay outward, and each will consist of three or four feathers, depending on whether a total of six or eight are being used. In either case, the yellow will be on the outboard side of the orange.

4.   Place a drop of cement on top of the thread friction base, hold the assemblies firmly in place, and affix them to the hook with the tying thread. Be sure to start with a turn or two of thread that is barely snug, and then progressively increase thread pressure with each succeeding turn. Complete the tie-on with several neat, contiguous wraps and a drop of cement.

5.   Next comes the palmer-wound collar. Choose two saddle hackles, one yellow and one orange. They should be wide enough so the fibers, when spread, cover the hook gape. Prepare them for tie-on by stripping fibers off the butts.

6.   Tie both hackle feathers in at the same time, securing them with several tight wraps. Bring the tying thread forward so it is out of the way. The two hackles can be palmered on at once; however, I prefer doing them separately to insure that both are wound tight to the shank and securely fastened. Grasp the foremost hackle stem near the tip with pliers and make two to four neat, contiguous turns. Secure with the thread and trim off the hackle tip.

7.   Grasp the rearmost or second hackle with your pliers, make one turn behind the previously wound hackle, and then proceed to wind forward through it one or two turns. Finish up with a last turn in front, secure it tightly in place, and trim the tip end close to the wrap. When winding the second hackle forward, try to avoid trapping the protruding fibers from the first hackle. Often this can be done by changing the tension with which you wind the second feather, rerouting it very slightly, or wiggling it fore and aft (with reference to the hook shank) as you progress forward.

8.   The fly is now complete unless the shank is to be covered with thread. In either case, a whip-finish and cement at this point are good insurance. If the hook shank is to be covered, continue winding the thread forward after completing the whip-finish in neat, contiguous wraps. Apply another whip-finish a short distance behind the eye, then cement all exposed thread.

The tail, or rear wing, tied in.

A palmer-wound collar is added.

The shank of the finished Shallow-Water Tarpon Fly is covered with thread. Note the splayed-out position of the tail.

ADDITIONAL OPTIONS AND COLORS

The Stu Apte Tarpon Fly is another good example of the lack of convention and formality surrounding saltwater flies. In addition to leaving the hook shank bare or covering it with thread, there are other commonly employed options: The bare shank may be painted fluorescent orange or red, the shank may be covered with thread and then painted, or fluorescent yarn may be used rather than thread. In addition, a painted eye is often added, in which case the thread immediately in front of the collar is built up to form a head, then tapered down to the shank and continued forward to the front of the hook. An eye is applied on each side of the enlarged area.

The same basic type of fly is also tied in many other colors, some of which have been given specific names. For example, a well-known pattern is Chico's (Fernandez) Shallow Water Tarpon Fly, which consists of an orange and grizzly mix in both the tail and the collar, with an orange hook shank.

Other popular color combinations in the Florida Keys are yellow-and-grizzly, blue-and-grizzly, and red-and-yellow. In Belize, one of the most popular combinations is red-and-black.

There is one other fly for shallow-water use that I should describe. It's not exactly like the fly we've just tied, but it is close enough that a verbal description will suffice. There are times when the fish tend to ignore or even flush from a brightly colored fly. As a result, a rather drab fly with a humble name was designed: It's called the Cockroach. The fly incorporates about six grizzly saddle hackles tied in at the bend to splay outward. Then a brown or gray bucktail collar is added behind the eye and tied in a manner to flow back to meet the saddle hackles.[1]

Just as in fresh water, local knowledge is highly desirable, and the prudent angler does considerable research before starting out on a lengthy and costly journey to far-off waters. The flies we've just discussed are all intended for use in the same basic environment: clear shallow flats. With them, an angler could fish the flats for tarpon any place, at the proper time of year, with a reasonable chance for success. On the other hand, these same flies would be lost in the discolored waters and heavy currents of Costa Rica's east coast rivers.

Let's take a look at a fly that's often successful under these latter conditions. The same colors that are used in shallow water are often used,

---

[1] One reference pictures this fly as having the tail feathers splay outward; others state that it is a Deceiver-type fly, meaning that the tail feathers would be tied in to stay together as a unit. In addition to bucktail, gray or red fox squirrel is also used for the collar. Various sources credit the fly to different originators.

A completed Cockroach.

but the flies are much more heavily dressed. As a result, they present a far more visible target, despite the water's squeezing action on them.

Bill Barnes of Casa Mar, one of Costa Rica's premier fishing lodges, often suggests grizzly-and-orange as a productive color. Inasmuch as Bill is a superb tarpon fisherman, I'd suggest we take his advice on our first deep-water fly.

THE DEEP-WATER TARPON FLY

GENERAL DESCRIPTION

The fly has a streamer-like configuration. It has a bucktail wing and underwing, both of which are fairly heavy and tied on a short distance behind the eye of the hook. Three or four saddle hackles are tied on each side over the bucktail to splay outward. Immediately in front of the wing there is a collar of palmer-wound hackle or marabou. In the remaining space, a pair of bead-chain eyes are secured to the shank.

The heavily dressed bucktail wing, and especially the underwing, minimize the possibility of the hackle feathers fouling around the hook gape. In addition, the splayed-out wings and the marabou provide breathing action while the bead chain helps bring the fly down and gives it a jigging action during the retrieve.

DRESSING AND COMPONENTS

Hook:	Mustad 3407 or 34007, 1/0 to 5/0
Thread:	Orange or black, 3/0 Monocord or 2/0 nylon
Wing:	White bucktail
Underwing:	White bucktail
Hackle Wing:	Four to six orange saddle hackles and two grizzly saddle hackles, one on each side
Topping:	Six to ten strands of peacock herl
Collar:	Orange marabou tied on to encircle the hook
Eyes:	Silver bead chain, approximately 3/16-inch diameter

TYING STEPS

1.　Place the hook in the vise and tie on behind the eye. Wrap the thread back in neat turns to a point short of the bend, and then bring it back to approximately 3/8-inch behind the eye. Be sure to leave enough room for the material plus the bead chain.

2.　Cut off a bunch of white bucktail for the underwing. The bunch should be about the diameter of a matchstick, and should be long enough to extend back one and a half to two hook lengths. Preen the hair as in previous flies. If you use a hair tamper, do so sparingly to maintain a tapered effect at the rear end.

3.　Secure the hair to the underside of the hook with several tight, neat wraps.

4.　Cut another bunch of white bucktail of about the same size, prepare it as was done for the underwing, and secure it to the top of the hook immediately over the underwing. The bucktail wings are now complete and in a position that allows plenty of room to secure the remaining materials to the hook without crowding. It should be noted that although the bucktail is tied on a substantial distance from the eye of the hook, that area will be hidden by the remainder of the material.

5.　Choose four to six orange and two grizzly saddle hackles. The orange should be long enough to extend approximately to, but no farther than, the ends of the bucktail, and the grizzly should be about one-quarter inch shorter.

6.　Prepare the hackles for tie-on as was done for the Sea-Ducer, and make up two separate assemblies. When tied on, the assemblies will splay outward and the grizzly feather will be on the outboard side of each.

7.　Affix the hackle feathers to the hook just ahead of the bucktail. The two assemblies will be secured in the same manner as the splayed-out tail section of the Sea-Ducer, except that they should be level or cocked

The bucktail wing
and underwing.

The hackle wing in
place.

The herl topping.

The marabou collar.

The finished Deep-Water Tarpon Fly with bead chain installed.

Note the heavy dressing and splayed-out wings of the finished fly.

upward slightly. If secured close enough, the bucktail tie-on area will cock the assemblies upward. You may have to take one or two wraps behind them to position them properly.

8.   When you're satisfied with their posture, secure the wing assemblies with several tight wraps, and apply cement.

9.   Secure the herl topping in place.

10.   Strip or cut several orange marabou fibers for the collar. Inasmuch as the marabou will slim down a great deal when wet, make the bunch fairly large and tie it in on the bottom of the hook under the point where the wing assemblies are secured. This can be done by holding the marabou under the hook or turning the hook over in the vise for the procedure. When tied on, the marabou is about one-half to three-quarters of an inch long.

11.   Gather an additional bunch of orange marabou fibers approximately the same length and secure them to the top and sides of the hook so the shank is completely encircled.

12.   Build up a base behind the eye of the hook with the thread. Fasten the bead chain with a series of figure-eight winds, as was done with the lead eyes for the Deceiver. Secure them with epoxy or super glue because the bead chain has a tendency to twist around the shank during fishing.

13.   Taper or smooth out the head, whip-finish, apply cement, and the fly is complete.

ADDITIONAL COLOR AND TYING OPTIONS

The deep-water fly runs the gamut in color, and is tied with many variations. Most flies of this type are the same as or a spin-off of Dan Blanton's extensive and productive Whistler Series. In addition to being called a Whistler, they are often referred to by one of several generic titles, such as deep-water fly or Costa Rica tarpon fly.

Silver or pearlescent mylar strips are often tied on each side, outboard of the hackle feathers, or on top of the bucktail wing. Topping may or may not be used.

Many tyers use two to four wraps of saddle hackle, palmer-wound, rather than marabou just forward of the hackle wings. Although some wind it so the fibers are perpendicular to the shank, I prefer that they lie back at about a forty-five-degree angle. The fibers then meld with the configuration of the wing, providing an overall minnow-like effect. This can be attained in two ways: One method is to force the hackle down by wrapping thread over the base of the collar; the other method is to fold the hackle prior to winding.

In order to fold a hackle, choose one that is soft and of the proper proportions. Strip the waste off the butt end. Grasp that end with hackle pliers and hold the pliers back in the palm of the hand so the thumb and index finger are free. If preferred, the hackle stem can be held in the tying vise, thus freeing the entire hand. Hold the tip end with the thumb and index finger of your other hand, pull the stem taut, and then, using the thumb and index finger that are free, fold the barbules down on each side of the stem. The feather will fold most easily in the direction of the natural curvature of the individual fibers, usually dull-side to dull-side. However, if the fibers happen to curve in the opposite direction, fold the hackle so the dull sides face out. This not only facilitates folding, but causes the fibers to curve in around the fly rather than splay outward.

When the folding is completed, tie the feather in with the barbules pointing toward the rear and the tip end under the hook. In tying in by the tip, the longer fibers near the butt end of the feather will be closer to the eye of the hook as the hackle is wound forward. While winding the hackle, continue to stroke the barbules toward the rear, preventing any of them from getting ahead of the stem. Many feathers do not fold well for their entire lengths. So be it! Just tie in additional feathers as necessary to obtain a full collar.

In addition to the orange-and-grizzly, Casa Mar also recommends red-and-white, red-and-yellow, and grizzly-and-yellow. I've also done well in the same area with brown-and-yellow and orange-and-black.

There is another option I would strongly recommend for fishing Costa Rica or similar waters: Use lead eyes in place of the bead chain. Lead eyes were not available when I last fished the area, but if I'm fortunate enough to get there again, I'll certainly have some flies weighted with them. They're available in a nickel-plated finish for those who want to stay with silver, or a lead finish that can be painted any color. The lead eyes help the fly sink faster, keep it down, and accentuate jigging action.

Hackle prepared for folding.

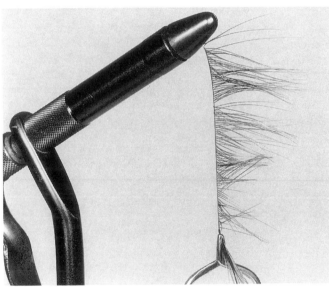

Folded hackle.

10

Bonefish Flies

Bonefish were one of the first, and still are one of the major species responsible for the popularity of saltwater fly fishing. To many, they represent the ultimate challenge. There are much larger fish in the sea, but very few are taken in the manner of the bonefish. It's a one-on-one situation with the entire scenario clearly visible to the fisherman. The experience consists of hunting for telltale signs, the stalk, an on-the-money presentation, and then refusal or a blazing first run.

Contrary to common belief, bonefish do not spend their entire lives on or directly adjacent to the flats; in fact, the International Game Fish Association all-tackle record of nineteen pounds was taken from the surf in South Africa. Bones are also caught trolling, and I've taken them on ⅝-ounce plugs while casting for other species. But these situations are not what most of us think of as bonefishing. The charm and challenge lies in pursuing the fish in gin-clear water that ranges from less than a foot to perhaps four feet in depth. The bonefish enters this environment to feed, and is very much aware of its vulnerability. As a result, it is often described as a bundle of nerves with fins. The slightest noise or out-of-the-ordinary movement, even the shadow of a bird overhead, will often cause one to flush. When it does, every bonefish in the area hightails it, much in the manner of a herd of whitetail deer escaping perceived danger.

As in most angling, the characteristics of the fish account for the challenges that are encountered and the methods used. The coloration of the bonefish consists of various silvery hues, making it difficult to see even in shallow water. As a result, its wraithlike comings and goings are responsible for its being called the Gray Ghost and the Phantom of the Flats. The muscular torpedo-shaped body accounts for its astounding bursts of speed, and the inferior placement of the mouth identifies it primarily as a bottom feeder.

The relatively small mouth is indicative of the size of forage bonefish normally consume. Although the diet consists of a variety of small minnows and worms, the mouth contains powerful crushers, rather than teeth, allowing the fish to easily devour shrimp, crabs, clams, sea urchins, and other crustaceans commonly found on the flats.

It is around these latter characteristics, along with the fish's propensity to feed in shallow water, that most bonefish flies have been designed. In fact, the majority are inverse-tied in order to minimize snagging—that is, the materials are tied on the bottom of the shank, causing the hook point to ride upright during the retrieve. In addition, the dressing normally shields the point, making the fly at least semi-weedless. Hooks are relatively small to accommodate the smallish mouth, sizes 2 through 6 are most popular.

Inasmuch as bonefish are constantly on the move, many patterns are tied with a weighted body to get the fly down to the fish in a hurry. This is especially true for fishing in more than a couple of feet of water, or fishing an area with a strong tidal flow, a phenomenon common to large tropical flats. The tidal range in some areas may be a foot or less; however, the shallow areas that are covered and drained during the flood and ebb are so vast that the water moves rapidly across them. Conversely, when fishing very shallow water—eighteen inches or less—it may be desirable to use an overdressed fly to retard the sink rate.

We'll tie three different patterns, all of which are popular throughout the bonefish belt.

THE CRAZY CHARLIE BROWN

GENERAL DESCRIPTION

This fly has been marketed by several commercial firms, but according to Eric Leiser, it is an adaptation of Bob Nauheim's original Nasty Charlie.

Like most bonefish patterns, the fly does not imitate any specific form of life. Instead, it is a general representation of the food typically found on a tropical flat.

The fly is an inverse-tie, using bead chain to provide a slight amount of weight while at the same time giving the appearance of eyes. The body is pearlescent mylar with an overwrap of a clear plastic such as V-Rib, Swannundaze, or similar material. The wing is brown hair cocked upward to cover the hook point.

DRESSING AND COMPONENTS

Hook: Mustad 3407 or 34007, #6 to #2.
Thread: 3/0 Monocord or 2/0 nylon, brown or white
Body: Pearlescent mylar with an overwrap of clear V-Rib
Wing: Brown calf tail
Eyes: Silver bead chain, ⅛-inch diameter

TYING STEPS

1. To make this an inverse-tied fly, mount the bead chain on what we normally consider the top of the shank to insure that the hook rides in the desired position. Place the hook in the vise in the conventional manner, and build a friction base.

2. Fasten the bead chain over the friction base with figure-eight windings. On a #6 hook, they should be placed about ³⁄₁₆-inch behind the eye to allow enough room to install the wing in front of them.

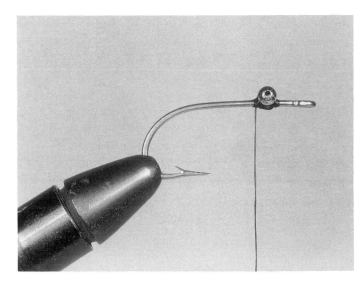

Bead chain is installed.

3.   Tie in the V-Rib behind the bead chain, then wind the thread back to a position slightly beyond the curvature of the bend.

4.   Wrap the V-Rib back to the same point, secure it in place, then position the excess out of the way. Bring the thread forward to just behind the bead chain.

5.   Secure the mylar at that point, then bring the thread forward of the bead chain, positioning it for final tie-off of both the mylar and the V-Rib.

V-Rib is tied in behind the bead chain; the thread is wrapped back into the bend.

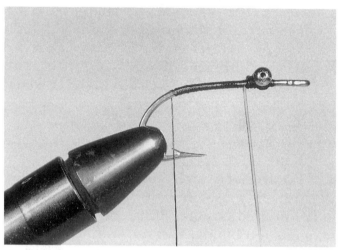

V-Rib is wound over the thread into the bend; the thread is brought forward to the bead chain. Mylar is tied in behind the bead chain, then the thread is brought forward of the bead chain.

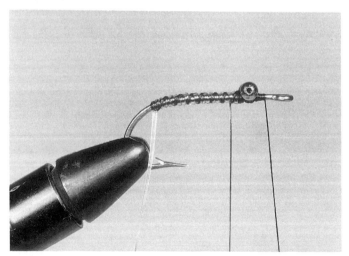

6. Wrap the mylar back into the bend, then forward over itself. Figure-eight it once to get it forward of the bead chain, then secure it in place.

7. Bring the V-Rib forward in contiguous wraps, figure-eight it once around the bead chain, and secure.

8. Now turn the hook over in the vise for placement of the wing on what we normally consider the bottom of the shank. Cut a bunch of calf tail approximately ⅛-inch in diameter and long enough to extend

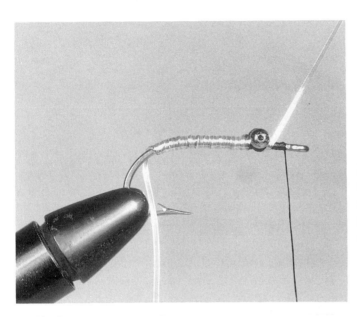

Mylar is wrapped to the bend and then forward to a point ahead of the bead chain.

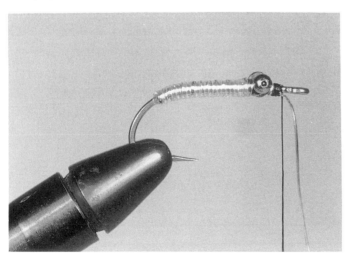

The V-Rib overwrap is wound on.

The finished Crazy
Charlie Brown with
wing installed.

beyond the bend a quarter- to a half-inch. Preen the hair, removing any
that are exceptionally unruly, and tie the wing in place between the eye
of the hook and the point at which the bead chain is secured. If necessary, take one or two wraps behind the wing to cock it up over the hook
point.

9.   Shape the head, whip-finish, and cement.

The Crazy Charlie is tied in a number of other colors, the following
being the most popular. Bear in mind that in each case a clear plastic
overwrap is used to cover and protect the mylar.

Pattern	Body	Eye	Wing
Crazy Charlie Pink	Pearlescent	Silver	Pink
Crazy Charlie White or Cream	Pearlescent	Silver	White or Cream
Crazy Charlie Brown (alternate)	Gold	Gold	Brown

THE BONEFISH SPECIAL

Our next fly is another Chico Fernandez creation. It is a pattern
that most veterans of the flats feel should be included in every
bonefisherman's fly box.

GENERAL DESCRIPTION

This fly is also an inverse-tie representative of typical forage found on the flats. It has an orange marabou tail and a gold body. The wing is grizzly hackle over white bucktail or calf tail.

DRESSING AND COMPONENTS

Hook: Mustad 3407 or 34007, #6 to #2
Thread: 3/0 Monocord or 2/0 nylon, black
Tail: Orange marabou
Body: Gold mylar with clear or gold monofilament overwrap
Wing: Two grizzly saddle hackles tied on top of a white bucktail or calf-tail wing

TYING STEPS

1. Mount the hook in the vise in the conventional manner, tie in behind the eye, and wind the thread back to the bend. The wraps should be neat enough to form a smooth base for the mylar.
2. Tie in a short section of orange marabou, extending beyond the bend approximately ⅛- to ¼-inch. Before bringing the thread forward, secure a length of clear or gold monofilament and place it out of the way in a material clip.
3. Bring the thread forward to a point behind the eye, leaving enough room in front for the wing. Secure a length of gold mylar to the shank, wind it back to the bend then back over itself, tying off at the starting point. Coat the hook and each layer of mylar with clear cement as the windings progress.

The marabou tail is tied in.

Monofilament is tied in at the bend. The thread is brought forward and mylar is tied on.

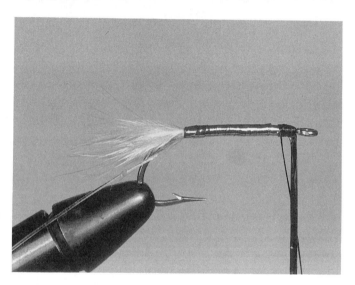

The mylar is wound.

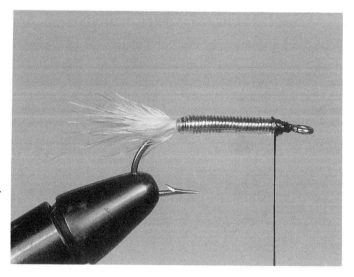

A monofilament overwrap is wound on.

The finished
Bonefish Special,
with hairwing and
grizzly hackle tied in.

4. Wind the monofilament forward in neat, contiguous wraps and secure it along with the mylar.

5. Now turn the hook over in the vise and tie the white hairwing in place. Immediately over that, tie in two grizzly saddle hackles. The feathers should not splay outward, but should be parallel to each other. The entire wing should be cocked slightly upward to shield the point, and should extend beyond the bend about half a shank length.

6. Shape the head, whip-finish, and cement.

THE HORROR

This pattern has withstood the test of time and is still as productive as it was when first introduced many years ago. It is often credited with being the first bonefish fly tied in inverse style, and was created by Pete Perenchief of Bermuda. The fly is very sparsely dressed, making it easy to cast and causing it to sink quite readily. Another decided advantage is simplicity and the ease with which it's tied.

GENERAL DESCRIPTION

The dressing is confined to about one-third of the forward portion of the hook shank, and consists of a yellow chenille body and a brown hairwing. Actually, the chenille body runs from behind the wing to a position forward of it, forming what might be considered a chenille head or collar. Recently I've noticed some tyers are adding a cree hackle feather to each side of the wing to provide the banding or the appearance of segmentation common to many small creatures found on the flats.

DRESSING AND COMPONENTS

Hook: Mustad 3407 or 34007, #6 to #2
Thread: 3/0 Monocord or 2/0 nylon, white or yellow
Body: Yellow chenille
Wing: Brown bucktail, usually the short hair from the top or side of the tail

TYING STEPS

1. This fly is so simple that the tyer may start with the hook in the vise in the inverse position. Secure the thread and build a friction base that extends from the eye of the hook rearward about one-third the shank length.
2. Tie on the bucktail wing about a quarter of the shank length behind the eye. The wing should be about twice the length of the shank.
3. Tie in the chenille immediately *forward* of the wing. Then take one or two turns of chenille *behind* the wing, positioning the hair to cover the hook point. Bring the chenille forward of the wing and build a head or collar over the windings that secure the wing in place. This portion of the fly will be approximately twice the diameter of the body behind the wing.
4. Secure the chenille, whip-finish, and cement.

THOUGHTS ON THE INVERSE TIE

The inverse, or reverse, tie is accomplished in several ways. Each method has its own advantages; the only common element is that the wing is tied on what we normally consider the bottom of the shank.

The most common method is to take a conventional hook and tie the wing on the bottom as described. This method depends solely on the dressing to create enough resistance to flip the fly over so the point rides in an upright position as the fly sinks through the water. A fly tied

The installed wing.

Chenille is tied in forward of the wing, and one or two wraps are taken behind the wing.

The finished Horror, with a chenille collar built forward of the wing.

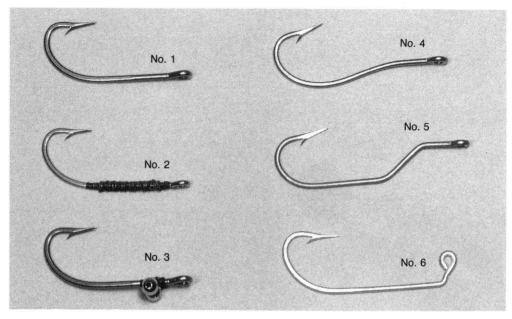

Inverse hooks. *Left, top to bottom:* plain hook; plain hook with lead-wire wrap; plain hook with bead chain attached. *Right, top to bottom:* bend-back hook; keel hook; jig hook.

in this manner is light and creates little disturbance as it enters the water. However, if it is very sparsely dressed, it may not always assume the desired position.

The other methods of executing an inverse tie involve changing the center of gravity of the hook to cause it to ride upside down. This is done by reshaping the hook or by adding weight to the shank.

The accompanying photo shows six hooks in inverse position. The first is a plain hook that will depend solely on the dressing to effect inversion. The next one has lead wire wrapped around the shank, and the next has had bead chain added. The two latter hooks will create a little more disturbance than the first hook when they enter the water, and will have faster sink rates.

The three remaining hooks have shanks that are shaped to influence the point to ride upright. The first of these is a bend-back hook, the next a keel hook, and the last a jig hook. The keel and jig hooks are purchased as is, whereas the bend-back is reshaped by the tyer. In shaping this hook only a slight bend is required; too much results in distortion of a fly's appearance. All three hooks as viewed from the side show the eye and point more closely aligned than in the conventional hook, thereby creating a more direct pull on the point during the hook-set. In spite of this, many tyers feel the hooking potential of the keel hook is enhanced by bending the point out slightly to compensate for the loss of gape created by the shank.

11

Permit Flies

Although I mentioned in the preceding chapter that many fly fishers consider the bonefish to be the ultimate challenge, I feel I can say with certainty that all *flats* fishers consider the permit to be the ultimate prize. That may sound controversial, but the difference revolves around the words "challenge" and "prize." There is no question about both species presenting a challenge, but as A. J. McClane stated in *McClane's Game Fish of North America*, "The permit is the rarest gamefish in the world purely in terms of how few are caught, as opposed to how many anglers cast to them." And bear in mind that the author was not restricting his discussion to fly fishing. Actually, so few permit are caught on the fly that many renowned fishermen feel the species should not be considered a viable or practical fly-rod target. Still, enough are taken to keep the undaunted feather merchant coming back.

The permit feeds on the flats, but because it's deep-bodied, it is normally encountered in water a foot or so deeper than that in which bonefish are found. It feeds in a manner similar to the bonefish, rooting around the bottom for the same basic types of food. It is exceptionally wary, has keen eyesight, and makes an extremely difficult target as it scoots about in erratic fashion. In addition, it apparently has an aversion to feathers—often following and sometimes bumping a fly during the retrieve, but not taking.

If the angler is fortunate enough to get a hit, his problems are just starting. The fish not only has a fourply mouth, but about the time a bonefish is ready to roll over and quit, the permit is just shifting into high gear. It makes exceptionally long runs and has a bagful of tricks, which include dragging the line over and banging its head on the bottom or rubbing its mouth in the sand to rid itself of the hook. Considering permit get much larger than bonefish, often weighing twenty to forty pounds or more, the angler has his hands full.

Very few fly fishers go out specifically for permit, but consider it an opportunity game. As a result, many keep a second rod rigged for permit while pursuing tarpon, bonefish, or other fish on the flats. This can be well worth the effort, because catching just one on the fly in a lifetime of angling is considered a noteworthy achievement.

After discussing the difficulties involved in taking a permit on feathers, I'm somewhat hesitant to call any specific fly a "permit fly." However, there are a few patterns that are starting to develop track records. By the same token, it should be realized that these same flies will certainly take other species. In fact, one of the patterns we'll tie, the Puff, is one of my favorites for bonefish.

THE PUFF

Captain Nat Ragland, a Florida Keys guide, originated the Puff, and it has probably taken more permit than any other fly. We'll start by tying an adaptation of the original Puff in a tan color. Although the original pattern was often tied using cree for the tail feathers, we'll use barred ginger because it is easier to obtain.

GENERAL DESCRIPTION

The fly is a general representation of life found on the tropical flats rather than an imitation of a specific organism.

Glass eyes are tied on near the front of the hook, not only for the appearance, but to provide some weight. The body is tan chenille, and the tail is brown calf- or bucktail flanked by barred ginger hackles tied to splay outward. Immediately in front of the tail is a palmer-wound collar.

The fly casts well and is nonfouling due to the placement of the tail. More important, it sinks readily because of the glass eyes and has a definite jigging action as it is retrieved across the bottom.

Dressing and Components

Hook:	Mustad 3407 or 34007, #4 to 1/0
Thread:	3/0 Monocord or 2/0 nylon, tan
Body:	Tan chenille
Hackle Collar:	Three or four turns of barred ginger hackle, palmer-wound
Tail:	Tan bucktail or calf tail flanked by two barred ginger hackles on each side, splaying outward; the tail is 1½ to 2 times the shank length
Eyes:	Orange or amber glass eyes, 4 to 6 mm depending on the amount of weight desired

Tying Steps

1. Secure the thread to the hook and build a friction base for the glass eyes.

2. Secure the eyes in the same manner as was used for the feather squid. Depending on the size of the fly, leave ⅛- to ¼-inch between the front edge of the glass eyes and the eye of the hook to allow the chenille body to be tapered down to the shank.

3. Wind the thread back to the bend and tie in a small bunch of brown calf tail or bucktail about the same length as the hook.

4. Tie in four barred ginger hackle feathers, two on each side of the tail, in such a manner that they splay outward. These are usually about one-half the shank length longer than the hair.

5. Immediately in front of the tail, secure one or two more hackle feathers by the butt ends and wind them forward palmer-style for three or four turns. These hackles should be wide and soft to accentuate movement as the fly is stripped through the water.

6. Bring the thread forward to a point just behind the eyes and tie in a length of tan chenille. Then bring the thread *forward* of the eyes. Wind the chenille back to the collar, then forward over itself, figure-eight it around the eyes, and then taper it down to meet the hook shank behind the eye of the hook.

7. Whip-finish and cement.

The Puff is tied in black and various shades of tan and brown, using brown, grizzly that has been dyed brown, and furnace hackle feathers in place of the cree or barred ginger.

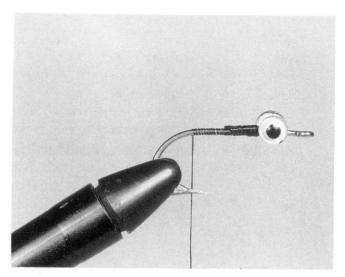

The eyes are in place.

The tail is tied in.

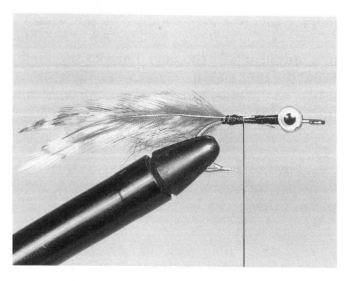

The hackle feathers are tied in on each side of the calf tail.

The hackle collar is palmer-wound, and the chenille is tied in behind the eyes.

The chenille is wrapped over the shank and around the eyes to complete the body.

The finished Puff from above. Note the splayed-out tail feathers.

THE SHRIMP FLY

The Shrimp Fly is tied in pink, and is one of the more popular colors for permit in the Yucatan. I've also used the pattern successfully in various colors for bonefish, sea trout, weakfish, and other species. The pattern we'll tie is very similar to the Pink Shrimp described in Eric Leiser's *The Book of Fly Patterns*. In constructing our fly we'll use a different method of forming the tail and the carapace, and the completed fly will have antennae, whereas the one described by Leiser does not. The basic pattern has been around for many years and has undoubtedly undergone many developmental changes. There are many varied methods of tying it, all of which give similar final results.

GENERAL DESCRIPTION

As the pattern name implies, the fly is tied to represent a shrimp. The body is of chenille and the legs are formed by palmer-wound hackle. Either bucktail or calf tail is used to form the carapace. Inasmuch as the tips of the hair that form the carapace extend beyond the eye of the hook, they are used for the antennae. The tail consists of tips of hair tied in beyond the bend so that they slant downward.

DRESSING AND COMPONENTS

Hook: Mustad 3407 or 34007, #4 to 1/0
Thread: 3/0 Monocord or 2/0 nylon, white or matching color
Tail: Pink bucktail, use tips only
Body: Pink chenille
Hackle: Pink saddle hackle with barbules at least as long as gape
Carapace: Pink bucktail
Antennae: Tips of the hair used to form carapace divided into two bunches, with each bunch cemented and drawn to a point

TYING STEPS

1. Secure the thread behind the eye of the hook and wind it back to a point about a quarter of the way into the bend.
2. Tie the tail in at the point where the thread ends so that it has a pronounced downward slant. The tail should be relatively short; only

The tail is tied in at a pronounced downward angle.

one-quarter to one-half the length of the shank. Use only the tips, and tie them in so that they fan out on both sides of the shank.

3.   Cut another bunch of bucktail, approximately ⅛- to ¼-inch in diameter, to form the carapace. Make sure it is long enough to not only cover the body when folded forward, but also to form the antennae. Tie the hair in by the butt ends just above the tail so that the tip ends extend *backward*. This entire bunch will later be pulled forward and tied down at the eye of the hook.

4.   Secure a pink saddle hackle by the butt end just forward of the bucktail, and then a length of pink chenille. Wind the chenille forward to form the body, being sure to leave enough room to secure the bucktail when it is folded forward.

5.   Spiral the saddle hackle forward palmer-style. The barbules that extend below the shank form the legs, and those that extend above the hook should be trimmed off.

6.   Grasp the bucktail that extends back beyond the hook, pull all the hairs tight, and then fold the bunch forward, securing it behind the eye of the hook. It may be helpful to wet the bucktail with the fingers to keep it together while folding it forward. The tip ends should extend beyond the eye of the hook approximately the length of the shank.

7.   Divide the tip ends into two bunches with the fingers or a dubbing needle, and figure-eight the thread around them to position as desired and keep the bunches separated. Apply a whip-finish around the shank of the hook *under* the antennae, just behind the eye, and then cement it.

8.   Apply cement (Dave's Flexament works well) to the two bunches of hair that form the antennae. Then, using your fingers, stroke each bunch forward to form a point, and the fly is complete.

Bucktail for the carapace is tied in. Note the tips pointing backward— they will be folded forward later.

Hackle and chenille are tied in at the bend, and the chenille will be wound forward.

The hackle is palmered forward and tied off.

The carapace is formed by folding the bucktail tied on in step 2 forward and tying it down behind the eye of the hook.

The bucktail that extends forward of the eye is divided in two, forming the antennae.

An alternate method of forming the antennae is to substitute two strands of monofilament for the tips of the bucktail. After securing the bucktail behind the eye of the hook (step 6), cut the tips off and tie in two lengths of monofilament so they extend forward of the hook an appropriate length. Prior to tying them in, the back end of each strand can be melted to form a small ball. The ball, which is positioned immediately behind the tie-down area, forms an eye as it locks the strand in.

This shrimp pattern is tied in a variety of colors. In addition to pink, I also tie it in tan, brown, and a silvery gray that has a translucent appearance in the water. These latter colors are more realistic than the pink, and in my opinion are far more productive. In order to add some flash to the fly, mylar is often used in place of the chenille.

DEER-HAIR CRAB

The first of these flies I was aware of was a Dave Whitlock pattern called a Salty Crab, first available five or six years ago. Now, however, there are many patterns available. Most are relatively new and were probably developed with permit in mind—a small crab about the size of a half dollar is one of the species' favorite food items. However, a good imitation will take many species of fish. I haven't had a chance to use them on the flats, but have taken school-size stripers on them in the Northeast.

Some tyers cover the entire deer-hair body, after trimming, with quick-drying epoxy and embed the legs and claws before the glue dries. The body may then be painted. Other tyers cover only the bottom, or belly portion, with epoxy or hot glue to anchor the appendages. The upper portion is then left as natural trimmed hair. The pattern we're about to tie will be this type. I first saw it used in the Florida Keys a couple of years ago, but don't know who developed it.[1] It's certainly a welcome addition to the many deer-hair crab patterns now available.

GENERAL DESCRIPTION

The fly is intended to be a lifelike representation of a small crab, and it fills that role remarkably well. Because crabs do not swim straight forward, but rather obliquely to one side, the fly is fashioned with the eyes and claws on the side of the hook while the long dimension of the shell runs the length of the hook. The carapace, or top portion of the shell, is natural-color deer body hair, and the belly is made of white or cream-colored hot glue. The legs and claws are tan rubber bands, and lend a great deal of animation to the fly as it is retrieved. The eyestalks are monofilament with the ends melted to form the eyes.

Lead eyes are tied on the bottom of the shank just behind the eye of the hook. Because they are partially hidden by the deer hair and the hot glue, they are relatively inconspicuous. Their purpose is to cause the fly to assume a diving position, the attitude an escaping crab takes as it heads for the bottom. Depending on the amount of weight used, it may be necessary to use a sink-tip or full-sinking line to overcome the buoyancy of the deer hair.

---

[1]George Anderson, in an article called "Permit" (*Fly Fisherman* Magazine, March 1991) credits himself, John Barr, and Jim Brungardt with having developed the McCrab Fly. The McCrab is tied inverse style. Except for that and other relatively minor differences, it is virtually the same as the Deer-Hair Crab. Anderson says that they used the McCrab in the Florida keys and gave it to friends and guides in the area.

DRESSING AND COMPONENTS

Hook:	Mustad 3407 or 34007, 1/0 to 3/0
Thread:	3/0 Monocord or 2/0 nylon, brown
Carapace:	Tan or gray deer body hair
Belly:	Cream or white hot-melt glue
Legs:	Tan rubber bands, approximately 1/16-inch wide
Claws:	Tan rubber bands, approximately 1/8-inch wide
Eyes and Eyestalks:	Monofilament, twenty-five to thirty pounds, preferably a brownish color

TYING STEPS

1.   Spin deer body hair on the hook from the bend to just behind the eye, as was done for the Deer-Hair Squid.

2.   Trim the deer hair so that, as viewed above the shank from the side and from the front, it forms a shallow crescent from front to back and side to side. Viewed from the top it is elliptical in shape but somewhat pointed at both the forward and rear ends. For a 2/0 hook, the body is about 1⅛ inches long and ⅞-inch wide. Below the shank, the body is trimmed as close to the hook as possible to allow for the addition of belly material, legs, and claws while creating as little obstruction as possible in the gape.

Deer hair is spun on the hook for the body.

A side view of the deer hair trimmed to form the body.

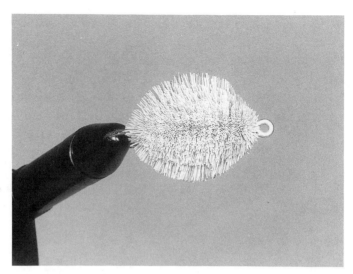

Top view of the body
after trimming.

3.   Tie the lead eyes on the bottom of the shank behind the eye of
the hook. Before securing them, slide them back into the deer hair to
position them inconspicuously. Then, working with the thread barely out
of the bobbin so as not to bind down the deer hair, figure-eight them in
place. The size of the lead eyes will vary with the size of the fly and how
densely the deer hair is packed. I usually use $\frac{1}{16}$- or $\frac{1}{10}$-ounce lead eyes
on a 2/0 hook.

Lead eyes are
installed on the
bottom of the shank.

4.   Apply a whip-finish behind the eye, and cement.
5.   Next comes the belly and the "hardware," that is, the legs, claws,
and eyestalks. Apply a thin bead of hot-melt glue around the bottom of
the fly about $\frac{1}{8}$-inch from the edge to form the periphery of the belly.
While the glue is pliable, embed the legs, claws, and eyestalks in their

A layer of hot-melt glue is applied to the bottom of the body, and two legs are embedded in it.

Additional glue is applied, and the claws, eyes, and remaining legs are embedded.

proper positions. If necessary, resoften the glue with the tip of the gun—just make sure additional glue isn't being fed at the same time.

6.   Fill in the center of the belly with additional hot glue, spreading and smoothing it as you proceed. If it is too thick in some areas, the excess can be removed by resoftening and then picking it off by rolling it onto a dubbing needle or a toothpick. Finish smoothing the surface with the side of the tip, and the fly is complete.

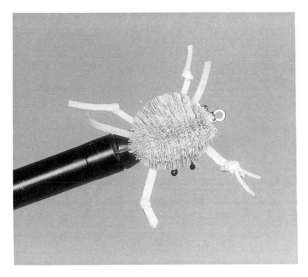

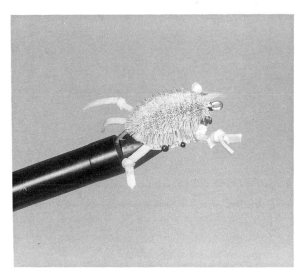

A top view of the finished Deer-Hair Crab.

Sideview of the Deer-Hair Crab.

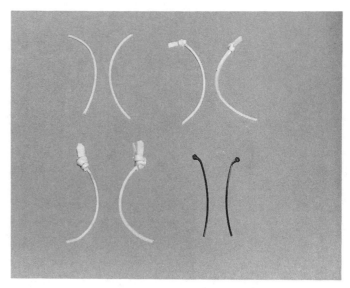

Legs, claws, and eyes, ready for installation.

NOTES ON EYES, LEGS, AND CLAWS

The eyestalks and eyes are formed by melting just the tip of a piece of monofilament so that it forms a round ball. The other end, which will be embedded in the glue, should be roughened to provide better adherence by squeezing it in the serrated jaws of a pair of pliers.

I install two claws and four legs, having found that more legs make the fly appear crowded and cumbersome. Although some tyers install straight lengths of rubber band for all of the legs and the claws, I prefer tying an overhand knot in two of the legs to make them appear segmented, like the swimmers on a crab. The method I use to make the claws is described in the following four illustrations.

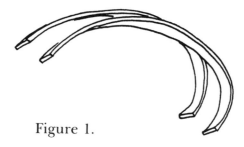

Figure 1.

Figure 1. Take two rubber bands and hold them parallel to each other.

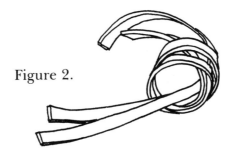

Figure 2.

Figure 2. Tie a single overhand knot as if both strands were one.

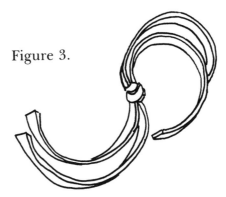

Figure 3.

Figure 3. When completed, there is a knot in the center of the paired strands.

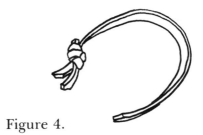

Figure 4.

Figure 4. Trim both strands on one side of the knot to imitate the upper and lower pincers of the claw. On the other side, trim one strand close to the knot, leaving the remaining strand to be embedded in the body of the fly.

It's a good idea to place a drop of epoxy, super glue, or Pliobond on each knot tied in the rubber bands to prevent it from loosening. I've found that about ³⁄₁₆- to ¼-inch of the rubber strand embedded in the hot-melt glue on the fly body provides a firm anchor.

12

Barracuda Flies

Everyone who has any intention of fishing the tropical flats should carry at least one fly for barracuda. This is a fish that has saved the day for many a frustrated fisherman.

Although the species is much maligned, many years ago someone had the good sense to name it great barracuda. I assume the "great" refers to the fish being one of the largest of its family. I like to think it refers to its fighting ability. When taken in shallow water on light tackle, the fish is absolutely spectacular. It can be extremely wary, is fast beyond belief, and its prodigious jumps would do justice to many an Olympian. If I didn't have *McClane's New Standard Fishing Encyclopedia* to back me up, I would be hesitant to write this, but the fish is capable of making long-distance leaps of twenty-five feet.

THE BARRACUDA FLY

This fly is like nothing ever seen in freshwater fly-fishing circles, and those new to the saltwater scene may wonder at its design. The entire dressing is tied in at the bend, and then the shank is covered with thread.

The fly is intended to represent a needlefish or balao, both of which are elongate fish with jaws that form a long beak. The thread-covered shank makes for a realistic imitation of the beak.

In his book, *Salt Water Fly Patterns*, Lefty Kreh credits Steve Bailey with tying a fly that is the same as or very similar to the fly we're about to tie. I tied an analogous pattern for many years, and was completely unaware of Bailey's design. His design may very well predate mine; this kind of parallel development probably exists much more than one would suspect.

The most effective technique for attracting barracuda with artificials is a very fast retrieve—a relatively simple matter with a plug-casting or spinning rod. Not so with a fly rod! Generally accepted methods of working a fly for barracuda are to place the rod between the knees and strip with both hands, or bring the fly back in fast, lengthy spurts by swinging the rod in an arc while stripping line with the other hand. Needless to say, both methods are tiresome, and the angler is often in a disadvantageous position when a strike occurs.

A definite advantage of this fly is its seductive action. Barracuda will often take it with a somewhat normal retrieve, albeit as fast as can be comfortably accomplished with rod tip and stripping action. It is usually tied with a wing, or tail, of blue over green over white.

General Description

The fly is elongate and very sparsely dressed, with all of the material secured just forward of the bend. Because of its length, usually seven to ten inches, FisHair is used for the dressing. After the material is secured in place, the thread is tapered down to the shank and then continued forward to completely cover the shank to just behind the eye.

The fly casts exceptionally well for its length because of the very sparse dressing, and the tail end of the FisHair is gathered together and glued or wrapped with thread to minimize fouling.

Dressing and Components

Hook:	Mustad 3407 or 34007, #1 to 3/0
Thread:	Red or light green 3/0 Monocord or 2/0 nylon; whichever color is chosen will be continued forward to completely cover the shank
Body:	None
Wing or Tail:	FisHair in three layers—blue over green over white—six to ten inches long and very sparsely dressed

TYING STEPS

1. Secure the thread at the bend of the hook and build a friction base for the wing.

2. Cut three bunches of FisHair—one white, one green, and one blue—and prepare each bunch by pulling out the exceptionally unruly strands. After preparation, each bunch should be about $\frac{1}{16}$- to $\frac{3}{32}$-inch in diameter when compressed between the fingers.

3. Tie each bunch on separately, as was done for the bucktail wing of the Glass Minnow. Secure the white immediately on top of the shank, the green next, and the blue last. Be sure to apply cement liberally between each layer, and cut the forward end of each on a bias to provide an evenly slanted surface running down to the hook shank.

4. Wrap the tying thread over the slanted area to provide an even taper down to the shank, and then continue the thread forward in neat, contiguous wraps to just behind the eye. Whip-finish and apply lacquer the entire length of the exposed thread. After it has dried, coat the entire area with epoxy to increase durability.

The wing is installed at the hook's bend.

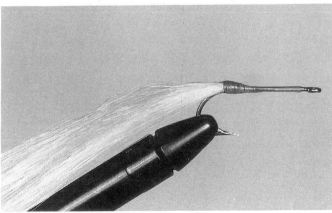

The shank is covered with thread to form a beak.

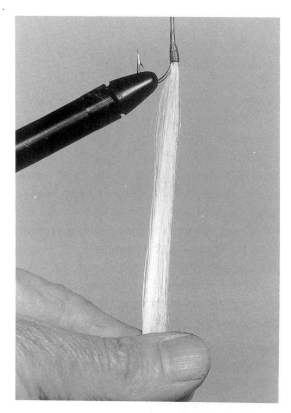

Glue is applied to the tail section.

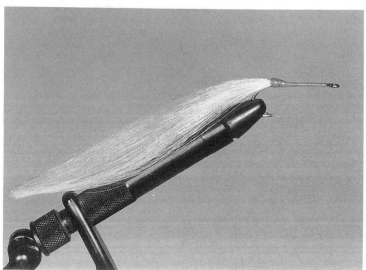

The completed Barracuda Fly.

5.   The last step is to cement the FisHair together at the tail. Secure the hook in the vise so the shank is pointing straight up vertically and the wing is hanging down. Use a fast-drying waterproof glue, such as Plio-bond. Place a little glue on thumb and index finger and smear it on the last ½- or ¾-inch of the wing to trap the strands of FisHair together.

VARIATIONS

The fly is normally dressed as described; however, it is also tied with a green over blue over white wing. Another popular color is all-orange. In addition, narrow strips of mylar are sometimes added to each side.

Some tyers also like to add a small doll eye or painted eye to the tapered area. To do so, it may be necessary to build the area up a bit with additional wraps of thread.

One other innovation is to tie the strands together to form a tail, rather than using glue. About ½- to ¾-inch ahead of the tail end, gather the strands together and apply ten to twelve tight wraps of thread, ending with a whip-finish. This procedure takes a little longer than the glue, but it causes the FisHair to flare out, making a more realistic tail.

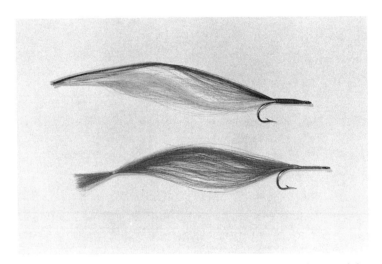

Two Barracuda Flies. *Top,* the tail has been formed by gluing the hair together; *bottom,* the tail has been formed by wrapping.

13

Tandem Trolling Flies

Trolling does not qualify as a legitimate means of fly fishing under International Game Fish Association (IGFA) rules. However, I can attest to its effectiveness from personal experience. I'm not an avid troller, much preferring to cast to a sighted target or to the potential lie of a fish, such as a jetty, piling, or opening in the mangroves. Even so, I don't believe in wasting precious fishing moments, especially when on a distant, somewhat costly journey. And when it's too windy or rough to fly-cast comfortably, or when I'm moving slowly from one flat to another, trolling can fill the void effectively. Through the years it's accounted for numerous snappers, barracuda, jack crevalle, cero, spanish mackerel, king mackerel, and other interesting species.

A tandem streamer is really nothing more than two streamer flies that are proportioned and color-coordinated so that together, one directly behind the other, they appear as one large bait fish. The problem lies not in the tying, but in joining the two hooks together. This can be accomplished in several ways, but there are a few points in the IGFA regulations that tyers should be aware of. This is not meant to imply that one must fish in accordance with IGFA rules, but most contests insist on this, and most anglers comply. It would certainly be a shame if a record catch were nullified because of a minor infraction of the rules.

The IGFA will not consider a fish that has been caught on a fly as a fly-rod catch if the fish was hooked while trolling. However, even if a streamer or popper is of tandem design, a fish can be accepted under the IGFA "Rules for Fly Fishing" as long as the fly was cast and the fish hooked and fought in a conventional manner. Flies dressed in that mode are commonly used in offshore fishing, where a long streamer or popper is cast to a fish that has been teased up to within a relatively short distance of the boat.

IGFA rules set the following criteria:

"A conventional fly may be dressed on a single or double hook or two single hooks in tandem. The second hook in any tandem fly must not extend beyond the wing material. The eyes of the hook shall be no farther than 6 inches (15.24 cm) apart. Treble hooks are prohibited."

To attach two hooks together, usually heavy monofilament is used—at least fifty- or sixty-pound test—or single-strand stainless-steel wire, or stranded stainless-steel wire (I use thirty-pound test). It's best to avoid light gauge single-strand wire because it kinks too easily—one fish often renders the fly useless. However, the heavier gauges, seventy or eighty pounds and up, can be used. In fact, if the fly is to be used for casting, the stiff single-strand wire is used by many tyers—the flexible connections, if too soft and of substantial length, allow the trailer hook to foul around the line or leader too easily. For very short connections, many tyers opt for heavy monofilament.

Hooks are normally positioned so that both ride with the points down, or so that the forward point rides down while the rear point rides up. Many feel that better hooking qualities are attained with the latter configuration.

Whether using monofilament or wire, single or stranded, one method for attaching the hooks together is to lay down a good friction base of thread the entire length of each hook shank. Then bind the mono or wire to the top of each shank with tight, contiguous wraps of thread. Finish by using super glue or a coating of clear epoxy.

Some tyers like to insure that the attaching strand is locked to each hook shank. This is easily accomplished by making the strand a little longer, so that a tag end of perhaps one-half inch extends beyond the bend of the trailer hook and the other tag end extends beyond the eye of the forward hook. After the strand is initially secured to both hook shanks, fold the tag ends back along their respective shanks and bind them down, locking the strand to both hooks.

If the fly will be used for trolling only, I use either monofilament or stranded wire—the type that is used for downriggers. The flexible connection permits some lateral movement of the fly, thereby increasing realism. In addition, I prefer doubling the strand; however, I sometimes wear both belt and suspenders to avoid the remote possibility of an embarrassing situation. I prefer the double strand because although I seldom troll, when I do it's in water where the bite is unpredictable—both as to species and size. The double strand obviously provides additional security.

In using the doubled wire (or monofilament) for attachment, measure the distance between the eyes of the two hooks, then cut the strand twice that length plus a couple of inches to allow for bending and ease of handling. Fold the strand in half, but do *not* kink it at the fold. The fine stranded wire will bend into a narrow U-like configuration. Pass both ends of the folded strand through the eye of the trailer hook from top to bottom. Bring the folded end back over the bend and then up past the point to the bottom of the shank. Slide the entire attachment forward until the fold nestles behind the eye of the hook.

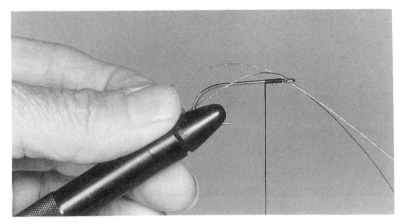

The wire is doubled and passed through the eye of the hook.

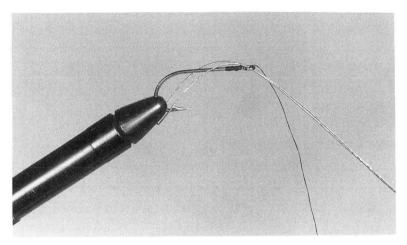

The doubled end of the wire has been passed down over the bend of the hook.

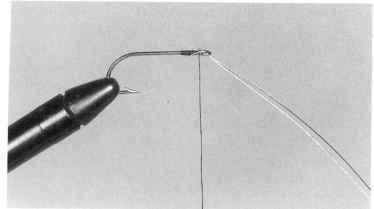

The doubled end is pulled up snugly beneath the shank and behind the eye of the hook.

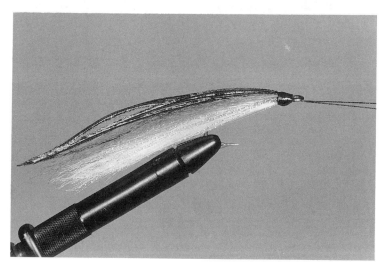

The trailer hook, completely dressed.

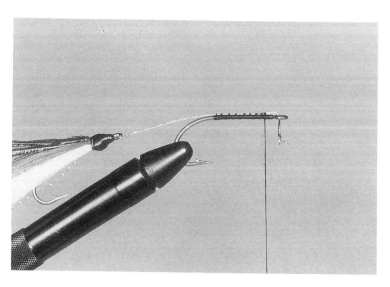

The doubled wire is secured to the top of the forward hook, its ends bent down through the eye.

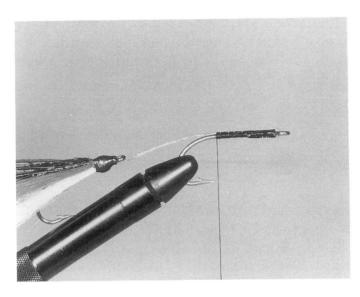

The wire ends are folded up under the shank and secured.

The attachment is secured to the forward hook after completing the dressing on the trailer hook. Build a threaded friction base on the shank of the forward hook and bind both strands of flexible wire to the shank at the same time. To insure their being locked in place, both tag ends of the attaching strands can be bent down through the eye of the hook and folded back along the shank, where they're secured with wrapping.

One other tip. When tying a tandem trolling streamer, use thread on the trailer hook that matches the color of the wing. Otherwise, when the streamer is wet, the head of the trailer will show through as a contrasting spot in the middle of the fly.

TANDEM TROLLING FLY

My favorite colored trolling fly is blue-over-white with herl topping, so let's follow that recipe for our first tandem streamer.

GENERAL DESCRIPTION

The fly is usually seven to ten inches long, and it can be tied so the points on both hooks ride down, or so that the trailer hook rides with the point up. In either case, the underwing is white and the overwing is two shades of blue, with the darker shade on top. Mylar, Flashabou, or Krystal Flash is used on the sides of both the forward and rear hooks, and a herl topping is placed on each hook. Depending on the length of the fly, use either bucktail or FisHair for the wings.

Aside from the attachment between the two hooks, the most important aspect of the fly is to proportion it so the wing on the forward hook blends and melds in with the dressing on the front portion of the trailer hook to produce a baitfish-like profile to the overall fly.

DRESSING AND COMPONENTS

Hooks: Trailer, Mustad 3407 or 34007, 1/0 to 3/0; forward, Mustad 3407 or 34007, 2/0 to 5/0

Thread: Trailer, medium blue, 3/0 Monocord or 2/0 nylon; forward, blue or fluorescent red, 3/0 Monocord or 2/0 nylon

Wings: Trailer, medium blue over light blue over white FisHair, with the white tied on as an underwing, five or six strands of pearlescent mylar are added to each side; forward, same as trailer, but usually substantially longer to cause it to meld with dressing on trailer

Topping: Trailer, six to ten strands of peacock herl; forward, same, but long enough to overlap the herl at forward end of rear hook

Tandem Hook: Attachment: stranded stainless-steel wire, single-strand stainless-steel wire, or heavy monofilament

TYING STEPS

Rather than detail the methods of winging the fly, an exercise that's been previously covered, we'll discuss those areas that differ from a conventional streamer fly, along with the sequence of assembly.

1. Place the trailer hook in the vise and secure the attaching monofilament or wire to the hook by one of the methods previously described.

2. Dress the hook in the conventional manner. Although the attaching strand will extend beyond the eye of the hook as much as several inches, working around it will become second nature. This is one pattern where using a bobbin with a long tube is a definite plus.

3. Remove the dressed trailer hook and secure the forward hook in the vise. Build a friction base of thread the entire length of the shank.

4. Take the dressed trailer hook and lay the strand (or strands) that extend from the front of it, on top of the shank of the forward hook and secure it to the shank the entire length of the friction base.

The forward hook, dressed.

The completed tandem trolling fly.

5. Dress and finish the forward hook in the conventional manner, making certain that the wing is proportioned to unite with the wing of the trailer hook.

ADDITIONAL OPTIONS AND COLORS

In addition to the blue-over-white wing, I also favor green-over-white, red-over-yellow-over-white, all-pink, and all-white. In all cases, I use herl for a topping and add some sparkle with mylar, Flashabou, or Krystal Flash.

In fishing the fly I use an intermediate-density or slow-sinking line, and find that the addition of lead eyes or glass eyes not only adds realism,

An alternate version: lead eyes are secured to the forward hook, and a head is formed with chenille wraps.

but aids in keeping the fly down in the surface chop. When adding the eyes, the appearance of the fly can be improved immeasurably by building a head of ram's wool or chenille around them, such as was done on the Sand Eel pattern. Eyes sticking out on each side of the hook shank remind me of a tiny hammerhead shark.

Another interesting and productive innovation is to tie the fly to imitate a needlefish or balao. In so doing, secure the dressing on the forward hook at the bend. Then install the eyes immediately forward of the dressing and build a head around them, tapering it down to a beaklike configuration to the eye of the hook.

14

Poppers and Sliders

Saltwater poppers, like their freshwater counterparts, are among the most popular lures in the fly fisher's arsenal. Fishing top water is not always productive, but a majority agree it is great fun. And if one sticks with it long enough, he or she will be amply rewarded. There are times when the fish turn on to poppers, and when that happens they often ignore everything else.

A saltwater popper is intended to imitate a hapless creature trying to escape danger, and the surface disturbance it creates makes it appear much larger than it actually is. As a result, it not only triggers a predatory response in a surprising number of species, but many of the fish taken on poppers are considerably larger than those taken on other artificials of similar size.

Baitfish that swim at the surface present elongated profiles and are capable of sudden bursts of activity, speed being their primary means of escape as they dodge about and skip across the surface. As a result, saltwater poppers are relatively long and slim: nothing fancy—just the popper body and a straight, lengthy tail of feathers, bucktail, or FisHair. Unlike their freshwater counterparts, there is no palmer-wound hackle, nor are there feathers splayed out to simulate kicking action.

Fortunately from the fly-caster's point of view, the slim profile is aerodynamically the better of the two designs. In general, the saltwater popper is considerably larger than that used in fresh water, and if it were dressed more extravagantly it would be extremely difficult to cast efficiently.

The most time-consuming aspect of making a saltwater popper is shaping, securing, and finishing the body. The tying skills involved are minimal, consisting of nothing more than securing a bunch of hair or feathers to the rear portion of the hook to form the tail. As a result, I'll dispense with most of the tying instructions and concentrate on body construction.

Before actually working on a popper body, take a look at a few design or construction techniques that will improve the popper's overall performance. A long-shank hook such as Mustad's 34011 or 92608 is used, with sizes 1/0 to 3/0 being most popular for inshore work. The tail is made one and a half to two times the length of the body. The hair should be evenly distributed around the hook shank to minimize fouling during casting. The long tail in conjunction with the popper body provides an elongated profile, and the long shank places the business end of the hook in a position where there is little or no interference from the body. In addition, the shank should be installed as close to the belly of the popper as is feasible. This not only makes the body float higher, but causes it to push more water when popped, and further minimizes interference in the gape.

Whether using a straight- or a hump-shank hook, the thread should be wound forward to the eye of the hook after securing the tail in place. This will provide a better surface to which the popper body can adhere. In fact, after securing the tail in place, I switch to heavier thread—A, C, or D—and then spiral it forward rather than wind it in contiguous wraps. If fine thread is used, and especially if the wraps are tight to one another, much of the glue is squeezed out when the body is forced into place over the shank. The greater-diameter thread permits a heavier glue line. This, along with the spiraled configuration, insures that a substantial amount of glue remains. And because epoxy doesn't shrink during drying, a firm bond is attained.

One more thing. There are times when the fish are feeding on or near the surface when a popper seems to turn them off, or may even scare them. Under these circumstances the fish will often strike a slider. A slider is made exactly the same as a popper except that the body is installed on the hook so that the narrow or pointed end is forward. As a result, it creates a wake but very little disturbance as it is retrieved across the surface.

Most popper bodies are made from cork; however, some of the synthetic materials available today are becoming increasingly popular. In fact, because manufactured foams are becoming so prevalent, we'll use them for our first popper body. They're not as durable as some of the other materials, but poppers fashioned from them are the quickest and easiest to make.

FOAM POPPERS

Many of the synthetics used are a form of closed-cell foam, and two of the most popular lures made from them are known as Evasote poppers and buoy poppers. The materials may be basically the same chemically, but Evasote is used primarily as a packing material, and buoy foam is obtained from lobster-pot buoy markers.

The foam materials are very light, making them relatively easy to cast. In addition, shaping the body is virtually effortless, because the material is easily worked with a knife or razor. A foam popper can be completed in a fraction of the time required to make a cork popper.

A cubed or squarish body, as shown in Figure 1, is easily formed with a knife. Cut out a small block of foam slightly larger than the intended size of the completed popper body. Cut the front and rear faces at a slant, then cut both of the sides at a shallow angle so the body tapers down slightly toward the rear. Rather than leaving the body square as viewed from the front, cut the two top corners or edges at a forty-five degree angle. This not only enhances the appearance, but decreases air resistance.

Figure 1.

If a cylindrically shaped body is desired, such can be formed by cutting a small plug from the foam with a cork boring tool or metal tubing such as electrical conduit or copper tubing. Make sure the cutting edge is sharp, and rotate the tool back and forth while pushing it through the foam. The front and rear faces of the body so formed can be left vertical or cut on a slant.

Whether the body is squarish or cylindrical, the final step is to install the *previously dressed* hook. Cut a groove in the belly of the popper or drill a hole to accommodate the hook shank. I usually bore a pilot hole with a small awl, spread cement on the shank of the hook, and then push it through the body from rear to front.

Most tyers leave the popper body its normal color, which is usually white or orange. Although the body can be painted, the air pockets in the surface of the foam are so large that a substantial amount of paint must be used to provide a nice finish—and paint adds weight.

I usually leave the body its natural color but tie several poppers with different-color tails to provide some variation.

KA-BOOM-BOOM POPPER

The majority of poppers are made from cork. One of them, the Ka-Boom-Boom Popper, is considered the standard for inshore fishing along the mid-Atlantic Coast. In fact, in that area its name is practically synonymous with top-water fishing. The Ka-Boom-Boom was originated by "Cap" Colvin of Seaside Park, New Jersey, many years ago, and he popularized its use not only for inshore fishing but also for fly-rodding the surf. His method of making the popper was passed on by his son to Bob Popovics, who continues to make it in the same manner. The only change Bob has made is to distribute the bucktail around the hook when securing the tail in place. He realized early on that this method of tailing would minimize fouling under the often-adverse conditions encountered when fishing off windy beaches with a fly rod.

The Ka-Boom-Boom is made from a cork bait-fishing bobber, commonly called a "perch float." The float is a modified cigar shape about 2½ inches long, and is available in varying diameters. Those that are ½-inch and ⅝-inch in diameter are probably the most popular for making poppers. Because the completed body itself is only about 1¼ inches long, two poppers may be fashioned from one float.

The float is cut in two at the appropriate angle so there is no waste of material. Two popper bodies, both the same length, can be completed. Although the face of the popper can be dished out in many ways, the easiest method, and one that provides uniformity in popper after popper, is to use a burr or a rotary file. When preparing the body to accept the hook, a hole is drilled through the cork or a slot cut in the bottom. In either case, the hook should be installed near the belly of the popper to cause it to float high, as explained earlier. The previously dressed hook is then covered with quick-drying epoxy and installed in the body. If necessary, fill each end of the drilled hole or the slot with epoxy after the hook is in place. Although the face of the popper is slanted, it is fairly close to vertical. This slight angle helps during the pick-up for casting, but still allows the bug to pop well. The greater the angle or slant, the easier the pick-up; however, if it becomes too great, the bug will not pop well and may even plane or yaw rather than pop. (See Figures 2–9.)

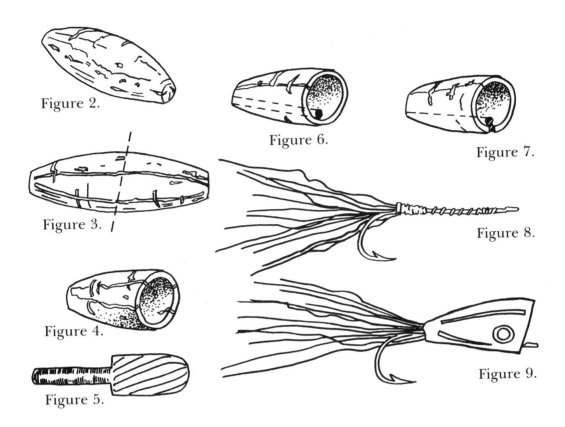

Figure 2.

Figure 3.

Figure 4.

Figure 5.

Figure 6.

Figure 7.

Figure 8.

Figure 9.

Last comes the finish, and here's where the tyer's imagination comes into full play. Although some display real touches of artistry, most salt-water poppers are painted a solid color, and white, yellow, green, blue, pink, and red are very popular. Several light coats are far better than one or two thick coats—thick coats add weight and are far less durable, tending to crack and chip with use. Pearlescent paint adds a nice professional touch, and many tyers sprinkle fine silver or pearlescent glitter onto the final coat as it is drying.

Most paint eyes on the body, but plastic eyes can be added, if preferred. Those with a stem on the back are especially attractive and durable. Just bore a small hole to accept the stem, and glue the eye in place.

LIVE BODY POPPERS

Live Body[1] is an expanded synthetic that is about the same density as cork. It is tough, resilient, and flexible, but firm to the touch, thereby adding realism. It is available in flat sheets, blocks, and cylinders of various diameters. There are seven different colors available, and although the white can be painted, this will add some rigidity to the material. The white accepts permanent-ink markers very well, and can thus be made any available color with no loss of flexibility.

Obviously, a cylinder is the easiest to start with when making poppers, and I'd suggest the ½-, ⅝-, and perhaps ¾-inch diameters for saltwater use. A plain cylinder can be mounted on a hook, but it will pop much better if one end is dished out, and will certainly look and cast much better if it is shaped similar to the cork popper just completed.

Live Body is easy to shape, and forms very rapidly when turned in a drill, Dremel tool, or other device. The key is to apply light pressure with sandpaper while turning at high speed. If you can find sand screen, it abrades much more rapidly than sandpaper. As the name implies, it is a screenlike material that is abrasive, and because dust falls through the screening, it doesn't clog as sandpaper does.

A screw is threaded through the cylinder. Because the sides of a sheet-metal screw are parallel, the screw is self-centering in the chuck jaws, insuring that it runs true. The screw is inserted in the chuck jaws, and sandpaper or sand screen is applied to the Live Body while the drill turns at high speed. (See Figures 10–13.)

Once the body is finished, the popper can be completed in the same manner as the Ka-Boom-Boom; just plug the center hole made by the screw with epoxy, silicone, or other flexible material. However, rather than making a fixed-body popper, we'll make a type that is commonly used offshore, a free-body or flexible popper. I've rarely seen them used inshore, but they are very effective there.

Once the popper body is completed, for all practical purposes the free-body popper is completed, as well. Leave the center hole as is, thread the leader tippet or shock leader through it, and then tie on a previously dressed hook for the tail. Slide the popper body down onto the eye of the hook or over the forward portion of the shank, and the popper is complete.

Any streamer-type fly in your arsenal, whether bucktail or feather, can be used for the tail portion. This versatility in changing the material, color, and size of the tail is one of the major benefits of using the free-

---

[1]Live Body is available from: Dale Clemens Custom Tackle Inc., 444 Schantz Spring Rd., Allentown, PA 18104.

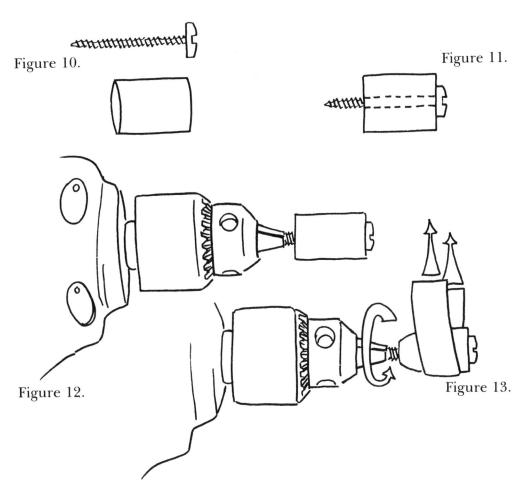

Figure 10.

Figure 11.

Figure 12.

Figure 13.

body popper. However, be sure to build up the head of the fly or a portion of the shank so the popper body is positioned where you want it. If there is no enlargement to hold it in place laterally along the shank, it will tend to slide back over the dressing when forcefully popped. This will not only spoil the dressing, but the popper body may be forced back far enough to interfere with the hook gape.

Another decided advantage of the free-body popper is the ability to change from a popper to a slider, and vice versa. Just reverse the body on the leader. (See Figures 14 and 15.)

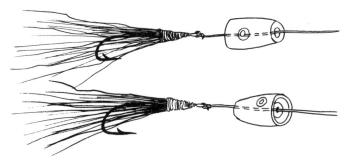

Figures 14 and 15
Free-body popper and slider.

Another technique worth trying is to peg or wedge the popper body on the leader an inch or two above the hook, using tapered toothpicks or plastic wedges similar to those used on popper corks. Although the lure will have a tendency to foul during casting, it appears to be much longer and is considerably more erratic during the retrieve.

With all these advantages, one may ask, why even bother with the fixed-body popper? Because there are disadvantages, too—just as in everything else, we must take the bad with the good. First, the free-body popper doesn't float as high as the fixed-body, and as a result, it may tend to dive when you pick up a long line. In addition, I've had the body work free from the hook while I was playing a fish and move up the leader until it was stopped by a knot, where another fish hit it. I didn't lose the fish I was playing, but if the second fish had been one of the toothy species, I'm sure I would have lost both the fish and the fly.

As to the previously mentioned tendency to dive, it is probably this attribute that causes the popper to track well, rather than skip around on the surface, as the fixed-body popper may do. And with a little practice, this tendency can be used provocatively during the retrieve—the popper can be drawn under repeatedly, emitting an enticing stream of bubbles on each dive.

One last thing before leaving the subject of poppers. Cork was used for a fixed-body popper and Live Body for a free-body popper for the sole purpose of illustrating two different materials and two distinct designs. The two materials can be used interchangeably with either design, and are equally effective. However, the Live Body is considerably more durable, even when subjected to the dentition of bluefish. In fact, for those who may wish to start their cork poppers from scratch, or those who may have difficulty obtaining perch floats, cork cylinders can be made into popper bodies in the same manner used to shape the Live Body. I prefer it to sanding by hand because it is so much faster and, once you become accustomed to it, so much easier to obtain consistent results.

15

Epoxy Flies

I like to think of the epoxy fly as the fly-rodder's jig. This fly is a relatively new innovation, and I'm sure many consider it to be the antithesis of the popper. Not only does the epoxy fly sink readily, but it is usually more fully dressed than the popper. In addition, it is dressed in a manner that causes the material to work and breathe as it is retrieved across the bottom. Rather than being streamlined, it is somewhat broad in relation to its depth, presenting what a fisheries biologist would probably call a flattened or depressed body form.

Demersal, or bottom-dwelling, fish, crabs, and other crustaceans may venture toward the surface in their quest for food. However, most are not built for speed and immediately head back to the bottom when they sense danger. That action is closely simulated by the epoxy fly as it dives for the bottom and kicks up puffs of sand or mud as it hops along.

The fly will take any species of fish that is susceptible to a lead-head jig, and is especially popular on the tropical flats. It has been responsible for the downfall of many large bonefish, and has really earned its laurels for the wily permit. With the exception of the Puff, it has probably taken more of this latter species than all other flies combined.

The epoxy fly has undergone a rapid evolution in design along with a proliferation of tying methods. Lefty Kreh, in his *Salt Water Fly Patterns,* states that development of the original fly is generally credited to Harry Spears of Marathon, Florida. In the beginning, the flies were painstakingly molded by hand as the material cured. Now they are made by more sophisticated and varied methods.

As with tandem trolling streamers and saltwater poppers, the tying procedures themselves are not new. Rather than repeating previously learned disciplines, I'll highlight the major tying instructions and then move on to body construction, as was done in Chapter 14.

THE EPOXY FLY—GENERAL DESCRIPTION

Because the epoxy fly is retrieved across the bottom, it is tied in inverse fashion. Standard-length hooks in sizes 2 to 2/0 are normally used. In order to control the sink rate and to insure that the fly rides with the hook point up, lead or glass eyes may be used, lead wire wrapped around the shank, or split shot inserted in the epoxy. In addition, although a conventional monofilament weed guard may be installed prior to making the epoxy body, the easiest method is to install two vertical strands of monofilament in the epoxy. They are positioned so that one is on each side of the hook and both are slightly ahead of the point. They are inserted into the epoxy before it sets up, and are of such a length that they protrude slightly above the point of the hook.

Another method of making the fly relatively weed-free is to tie on the dressing in such a manner that it shields the hook point, as was done with the bonefish flies. To do so, install the epoxy body far enough back on the shank to allow the dressing to be tied on behind the eye of the hook.

The conventional dressing for epoxy flies usually consists of a half-dozen strands of mylar or Krystal Flash tied in to extend straight back from the bend. One or two saddle hackles are then tied on each side to splay outward, and a palmer-wound collar may be added over the area where the tailing materials are secured. Some patterns are tied with marabou rather than saddle hackle. Colors run the gamut; however, browns and tans are probably most popular.

When the materials are secured behind the body, most tyers complete the dressing and then install the epoxy body, allowing it to cover and protect the tying thread.

MOLDING METHOD

Although it initially requires the greatest preparation, those who tie a substantial number of epoxy flies find that, in the long run, it is easiest to first produce a mold for the body. Instructions and supplies for making molds are available in most craft shops. Molding plaster is one material that is commonly used.

Although it may be more difficult to find, Rapid Stone is another molding material that may be used for epoxy flies. It is similar to plaster but sets up more slowly, making it easier to work with. No matter which material is used, it is a good idea to use a releasing agent in the portion of the mold in which the epoxy will be cast. This will allow the completed body to be removed from the mold without damage. Spray silicone can be used, as can a very thin coat of Vaseline. I normally apply the Vaseline with a Q-tip to insure a smooth coating; otherwise, the epoxy body will show any imperfections present in the surface of the Vaseline.

A completed epoxy fly or a lead wiggle jig can be used to make the mold. On the other hand, if the tyer wants to start from scratch, or if a unique size or shape is desired, the pattern can be shaped first in masonite or similar material. Because the epoxy will be cast around the hook, be sure to allow for the shank when making the mold, and also for any other components the mold must accommodate, such as glass or lead eyes. With reasonable handling, a mold will last for a long time; however, it is a good idea to make several so that a number of flies can be made at the same time.

Once the mold has been completed, tying skills again come into play, at least for the next two or three steps, as shown in the following illustrations.

After completion of the mold, the eyes are secured to the hook shank. Glass eyes have a wire stem on the backs and are secured by wrapping the wire around the hook shank, as shown. Lead eyes are secured with tying thread. The tail is tied in place, and the hook, with dressing and eyes in place, is placed in the mold. The body portion of the mold is then filled with epoxy, either with a syringe or by allowing the epoxy to run off the end of a dubbing needle. Once the epoxy has hardened, the completed fly can be removed from the mold. Note the monofilament weed guards that are inserted into the body before the epoxy sets up completely. (See Figures 1–4.)

Many tyers use quick-drying epoxy for the body because it cures rapidly; however, there are several other materials that can be used. Among these are regular epoxy and some of the two-part rod-finishing materials. I make some of my flies with liquid latex; it doesn't have the translucent appearance of the others, but it is soft to the touch.

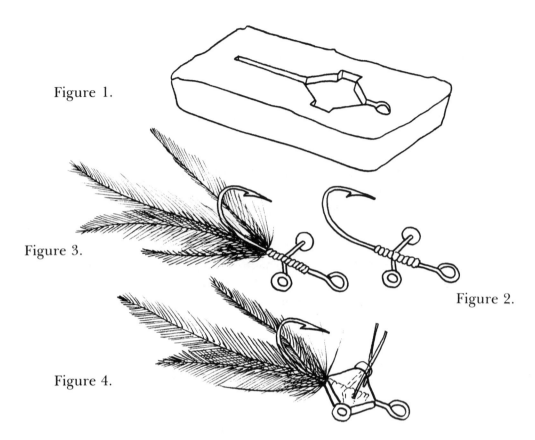

Figure 1.

Figure 3.

Figure 2.

Figure 4.

Usually epoxy bodies are left their natural colors, but they can be painted. In addition, while mixing the epoxy, glitter can be added, and there are epoxy dyes available. I've used liquid food coloring in the quick-drying epoxies with good results. It doesn't take much, however, so use dye judiciously.

ROTATING METHOD—USING FLEX COAT

A completely different way of making an epoxy fly is practiced by Jack Fragomeni of Cohoes, New York. In addition to being a very talented tyer, Jack is a licensed New York State fishing guide, a professional musician, and a teacher of music at one of the colleges in Albany. Jack has tied flies professionally and has fished upstate New York's lakes and rivers with a fly rod for many years. He also makes regular forays to the salt, including an annual trip to the Florida Keys.

The method Jack uses does not require the use of a mold. He dresses the hook and ties lead eyes in place. Then he uses Flex Coat, a two-part polymer rod-wrapping finish, for the body material. After mixing it, he lets it set for about forty-five minutes, or until it thickens considerably. Using a syringe, Jack applies a glob of material to the top and bottom of the shank at the point where the crossbar of the eyes crosses the hook. Jack then rotates the fly for an hour or so, using a rod-drying motor. This prevents the material from sagging and causes it to be distributed symmetrically around the shank and in the space between the eyes. He has adapted the rod dryer to accommodate up to fifteen flies at one time by using a cork arbor. (See Figures 5 and 6.)

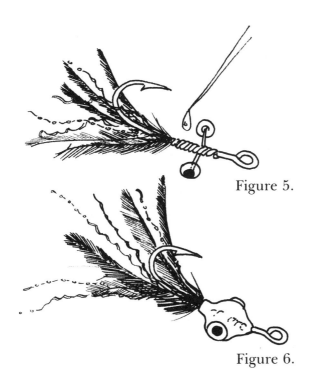

Figure 5.

Figure 6.

The amount of epoxy material applied will vary with the size of the fly desired, the distance between the eyes, and their size. However, if too little is used to complete the fly in one operation, the body can be built up to the desired size by applying successive layers. In fact, when using large glass eyes or when making a larger fly, that is the procedure I follow.

ROTATING METHOD—USING QUICK-DRYING EPOXY

The fly can also be made with quick-drying epoxy instead of Flex Coat, but because the epoxy sets up rapidly, it is difficult to make more than one fly at a time. But no special equipment is needed, and the fly is completed in a matter of minutes.

The hook is dressed and the eyes secured in place. Apply several drops of epoxy with a dubbing needle. Hold the hook by the bend and rotate it, orienting it in different positions to control the flow of epoxy. This will distribute the epoxy and prevent it from sagging. In two or three minutes the material will have set up to the extent that it no longer flows. Put it back in the vise to finish curing, and the fly is complete.

EPOXY-STRIP METHOD

Another method was (to the best of my knowledge) developed by Lefty Kreh, and is probably the easiest way to make an epoxy fly. It involves the use of epoxy strips, also called plumber's epoxy. Both the resin and the hardener are solid strips of a claylike consistency, and each strip is a different color. Equal portions of each strip are kneaded together until a uniform color is attained and then are molded around the hook by hand. The periphery of the body can be shaped with a knife, while the edges, top, and bottom can be smoothed with the side of the blade. The knife blade will cut and smooth better if it's first dipped in lacquer thinner. Water is also satisfactory, but it doesn't smooth as well as the thinner. If the completed body has a tendency to stick to the surface on which you're working, use waxed paper or aluminum foil under it.

HOT GLUE FLIES

Many tyers use hot-melt glue to fashion flies that are similar to those made of epoxy—they are called Hot Glue Flies. A small pool of molten glue is dropped on the work surface, which can be covered with waxed paper or aluminum foil. While the glue is soft, the hook is embedded in it. Then, as the glue cools, the body is shaped by hand or with a knife or scissors—either will cut the material, even after it has solidified. The edges of the body can be rounded and any irregularities smoothed by reheating the glue gun and using the side of the tip. I've made several in epoxy molds, and have had no difficulty as long as I used a releasing agent. The molten glue does have a tendency to trap air bubbles against the surfaces of the mold, but it's an easy matter to smooth out the imperfections the bubbles cause with the reheated glue gun.

Many tyers, myself included, have been surprised that epoxy or hot glue alone (that is, with no additional weight) molded to the hook is usually not enough to insure that the fly will ride in inverse fashion. The materials are just not as heavy as they appear. It is almost always necessary to weight the body with lead wire, split shot, or lead or glass eyes.

SAFETY

As we bring the tying instructions to a close—not only for the epoxy flies but for all the patterns—I should mention an issue of some general importance: safety.

Having been involved in safety engineering a substantial part of my life, I feel obligated to issue at least a mild word of caution. When using the various glues, lacquers, and solvents, be sure to follow the manufacturer's instructions. Use adequate ventilation, be aware of the potential fire hazard, and avoid excessive skin contact. Many chemicals are readily absorbed through the skin, and some, such as many epoxy resins, are known to be potential skin sensitizers. If there is any likelihood that young children may be around, keep all chemical products out of their reach. And be sure they cannot get at your tools—knives, scissors, razor blades, dubbing needles, and the like.

16

Random Notes and Conclusions

I hope that those of you who have read this far have every intention of tying several, if not all, of the flies detailed in the text. Anyone who masters the techniques outlined in the various chapters will be well equipped to master any technique used in saltwater fly tying today. Just as important, I hope you intend to use your flies at the first opportunity. They form the nucleus of a good selection for inshore waters anywhere in the world. In the larger sizes, many of the patterns are effective on offshore species.

If you're anything like me, you never tie just one of a given pattern. I'm so positive a particular fly is so irresistible to the intended quarry that I need at least three of each color for each fishing venture: one in the event of a break-off, one for the fish to wear out, and one so that I can continue catching fish after the first two are useless or lost. Sometimes I really do use all three, but never as often as I would wish. However, when I'm tying, especially for a specific trip, I'm always absolutely certain I will. That's the magic of fly tying and fly fishing—the optimism, the anticipation, and the satisfaction derived by the fully involved individual.

One may wonder why a person would tackle the salt with a fly rod. Not many years ago there were many seasoned fishermen who considered it a stunt. But every year many fish well over a hundred pounds are taken from salt water on flies. Even today, it's not uncommon for some fishermen to look at a saltwater fly rodder somewhat askance. I recently had one tell me he never heard of saltwater fly fishing, and another told me he didn't believe enough flies hatched in salt water to make it worthwhile. Each of these gentlemen fish frequently, and both live considerably less than a day's drive from some of the best waters on the Northeast Coast.

The point is that there are many active fishermen who are completely unaware of the resource, and countless others who are aware of it but hesitant to try it, even though seventy percent of the earth's surface is covered with salt water. Only three percent of the earth's water is fresh, and two-thirds of that, in glaciers and ice caps, is inaccessible. One who plies sweet water only is restricting his or her tying and fishing to a very small portion of what is available. Although the saltwater resource is far from untapped, even in heavily fished waters one can find plenty of elbow room. And, of course, the oceans and their coastlines are so vast that many areas are seldom fished, while others, I'm sure, have never seen a fly.

The burgeoning interest in saltwater fly tying and fishing has spawned the development of new tackle, tools, and materials. A great deal of this development has been the direct result of the involvement of fly tyers. Most tyers are innovative, and, being dedicated, they are constantly on the lookout for something new. In fact, many of the tools and materials in common use today are items an inquisitive tyer originally appropriated from a hobby shop, variety store, or some attic, closet, or work area at home.

In spite of the increased interest and progress in recent years, much of the ocean and many of the skills of fly tyers remain untapped. The ocean is so vast and the number of species therein so diverse that most knowledgeable fly fishers consider it the last frontier. Come join us! There's an ocean of challenge and excitement ahead.

BIBLIOGRAPHY

BAY, KENNETH E., and HERMANN KESSLER. *Salt Water Flies*. Philadelphia: Lippincott, 1972.

BOYLE, ROBERT H., and DAVE WHITLOCK. *The Fly-Tyer's Almanac*. New York: Nick Lyons Books, 1975.

FLICK, ART. *Master Fly-Tying Guide*. New York: Crown, 1972.

INTERNATIONAL GAME FISH ASSOCIATION. *World Record Game Fishes*. Fort Lauderdale: IGFA, 1991.

KREH, LEFTY. *Fly Fishing in Salt Water*. New York: Crown, 1974.

———. *Fly Fishing in Salt Water,* revised edition. New York: Nick Lyons Books, 1986.

———. *Salt-Water Fly Patterns*. Fullerton, Calif.: Maral, Inc., 1989.

LEISER, ERIC. *The Book of Fly Patterns*. New York: Alfred A. Knopf, 1987.

LEONARD, J. EDSON. *Flies,* 1988 edition. New York: Nick Lyons Books, 1988.

McCLANE, A. J. *New Standard Fishing Encyclopedia*. New York: Holt, Rinehart and Winston, 1965.

McCLANE, A. J., AND KEITH GARDNER. *Game Fish of North America*. New York: Times Books, 1984.

STEWART, DICK. *The Hook Book*. Intervale, N.H.: Northland Press, 1986.

TALLEUR, RICHARD W. *Mastering the Art of Fly-tying*. Harrisburg, Penn.: Stackpole, 1979.

———. *The Fly Tyer's Primer*. New York: Nick Lyons Books, 1986.

———. *The Versatile Fly Tyer*. New York: Lyons & Burford, 1990.

INDEX